The Toll House

The Toll House

MICHAEL & AUDREY WARD

2011
THE MEDLAR PRESS
ELLESMERE

Published by The Medlar Press Limited,
The Grange, Ellesmere, Shropshire SY12 9DE
www.medlarpress.com

ISBN 978-1-907110-18-4

The black and white line illustrations used in this book
are by the 18th century engraver W.H.Pyne.

The Author and Publishers have made every attempt to contact
copyright holders but if they have inadvertently overlooked any
they will be pleased to make the necessary arrangements.

Designed and typeset in 11 on 13 point Bembo Roman
Produced in England by the Medlar Press Limited, Ellesmere, England.

Contents

Toll Houses in England

Toll Houses in Wales

Preface

Several years ago when retirement brought the opportunity to travel through England and Wales the idea of creating a book was nowhere in our minds, but an interest in buildings and the history of our land led us to photograph some small, interesting houses that jutted on to the road throughout the country. Gradually this led us to investigate further a whole era of burgeoning change in our industrial history some 250 years ago, revealed by tracing the rapidly expanding turnpike road system set up between 1700 and 1850, when many toll houses were erected by private sponsors of trusts specially authorised by Parliament for the purpose of collecting money to pay for an improved road system.

While some authorities have recognised that a national schedule of toll houses should be made and kept for posterity, enquiries in record offices, councils and libraries showed sparse knowledge of these symbols of the amazing economic growth in Great Britain at that time. This led us to make our own record of them over a period of several years, photographing more than 300 of the more attractive examples. However places change, including names of properties and layouts of roads, making identification of remaining toll houses quite difficult. We have been fortunate that during publication of this book we came across a very useful website by Alan Rosevear, called *www.turnpikes.org.uk*. The site provides invaluable details of English turnpikes, toll houses and milestones. On it is a list of around 1,770 surviving English toll houses, by county, giving a unique national identity number to each property. With Alan's kind permission we have referred to this list for most of the toll houses in this book.

The discovery of such a wonderful historic legacy added a new dimension to retirement, and it is hoped the following pages will give pleasure to all who enjoy travel and looking at old buildings.

Michael & Audrey Ward

Publisher's Acknowledgements

The publishers would like to thank the following for their help
in the preparation of this book: Alan Rosevear for access to his wonderful
website; Katrina Dewar, and Connie and Grace Ward-Allen - for all their
dogged help in double-checking all the toll house names and references.

Introduction

Mention in the media nowadays of trouble on the roads can evoke a feeling of gloom and despondency for travellers, and solving the country's transport problems has become a hot potato in politics today. It would not have been any less so in the 18th and 19th centuries when road conditions were very different.

In the first centuries AD the Romans left Britain a strategic framework of roads many of which can still be traced along highways, such as Watling Street and Fosse Way, and many form part of the road system in use today. In his *Tour Through the Whole Island of Great Britain* Daniel Defoe wrote:

The causeways and roads, or streetways of the Romans, were perfect solid buildings, the foundations were laid so deep, and the materials so good, however far they were oblig'd to fetch them, that if they had been vaulted and arch'd, they could not have been more solid: I have seen the bottom of them dug up in several places, where I have observ'd flint stones, chalk stones, hard gravel, solid hard clay, and several other sorts of earth, laid in layers, like the veins of oar in a mine; a laying of clay of a solid binding quality, then flint-stones, then chalk, then upon the chalk rough ballast or gravel, 'till the whole work has been rais'd six or eight foot from the bottom; then it has been covered with a crown or rising ridge in the middle, gently sloping to the sides, that the rain might run off every way, and not soak into the work: This I have seen as fair and firm, after having stood, as we may conclude, at least 12 or 1600 years, as if it had been made but the year before.

In the period following the Roman occupation, the increasing trade in livestock led to the movement of large herds of cattle, sheep, pigs and even geese over the Welsh hills to eastern England. They would be driven for several weeks on their journey to the markets, accompanied by drovers riding ponies - the noise would have been considerable! The routes, through wild and lonely country, would have been hazardous, and in the days before banking, when many drovers carried sums of money on behalf of clients, they were prey to brigands lurking in the mountains and forests. Driving beasts over difficult terrain called for great skill, and drovers were often accompanied by other travellers who sought the benefit of their experience. Because travel was extremely dangerous there was little communication between people living in small hamlets and it was the drovers, who became some of the best informed men in Wales, who brought news of people and events in other parts of the country, and even the world. Welsh drovers preferred ancient ridgeways and upland routes which were free of settlements, wagons and crops, and would choose cross-country routes to make it easier for their herds to graze as they made their leisurely way to market in order to arrive in good condition. However, sometimes main roadways were unavoidable and this caused chaotic conditions.

Pilgrims on their way to or from monasteries established other routes and many roads were maintained by the monks to facilitate the industries and trade built up by their wealth. Kings and rulers were constantly on the move round the country collecting taxes and dues from their people, and would be accompanied by a retinue of carts and wagons filled with all that a royal personage required, including clothing and food for long periods away, as well as their treasury. Despite centuries of neglect many of these routes came to be regarded as 'royal roads' though they were little more than dirt tracks, often impassable in wet weather when they became quagmires.

With no one to take responsibility for the upkeep of roads and tracks, and with robberies and violence in the darkest regions, travellers had to be brave indeed. Great numbers of men were employed along the main routes to clear away fallen trees and to hew stones to fill the deepest ruts, but conditions must have been unbearable. When it seemed that road maintenance was failing to keep pace with the needs of increasing traffic, Parliament passed an Act making each parish responsible for the roads within its boundaries. Meetings were called annually to elect two honest persons to be surveyors, to keep records of work done, and often it was the farmers and innkeepers who were chosen because of their knowledge of local roads. The Act laid down that 'every person with land valued at over £50 must send a wain or cart with oxen, horses or other beast, and all other necessities to carry things convenient for that purpose, and also two able men with same'. Money for materials came from fines charged if labourers or teams did not appear.

The Act was very harsh. Every householder and labourer had to work on the road or send someone in his stead, for eight hours on four days a year as required by the surveyors. Later this was increased to six days a year. By 1670 fines were fixed at one shilling and sixpence a day for a labourer, three shillings for a man with a horse, while the absence of a cart with its two attendant labourers led to a fine of ten shillings a day. The modern equivalent would seem draconian! Inevitably the work was done with reluctance and without much skill, and often with rapidly disintegrating materials such as wood, faggots and even dung. People living in areas adjacent to industrial work began to object to the unfair burden imposed by the Act.

In the 17th century the justices of Hertfordshire, Cambridgeshire and Huntingdon turned in desperation to Parliament which came to their aid with the 1663 Turnpike Act. This permitted the collection of tolls from travellers along their section of the Great North Road. Gates were set up to halt traffic, and money raised by the tolls was to be used for repairs and improvements. Justices of the peace were to oversee the collection of monies and surveyors were to ensure it was properly applied. Further Acts authorised the collection of tolls in other parts of the country, and in the early 18th century bodies of trustees were appointed in place of the justices.

Thus a network of turnpike roads was set up. The Inclosure Acts of the 18th century forced traffic to keep to roads and prevented travellers from straying over adjoining common land to avoid payment.

The term 'turnpike' is thought to have originated from the 'gates' that were set up using horizontal tapering bars of iron or wood turning on a post with vertical pikes, or spikes. Until dues were paid these pikes could not be made to turn. The bars would have been merely functional in design at the start, later becoming quite ornamental in some cases. 'Pikemen' were the appointed toll collectors levying unpopular charges from a wide variety of road users, and they tended their gates at all hours of day and night. They were often subjected to harassment and verbal abuse, even violence - an older version of today's traffic wardens, perhaps! It is probable the pikes, or gates, were guarded from small shelters or huts in the early days, until toll-keepers were provided with converted cottages already at the roadside. As traffic increased purpose-built houses were provided by the Trustees, often of similar design but with variations in materials according to local tradition. Inevitably the cottages were a very mixed collection, some very simple and mean, without a garden; others, perhaps at the request of one of the Trustees, mimicked the local manor house in the style of an entrance lodge. Materials used were those locally available, such as stone, timber, wattle and daub and brick, with thatch, slate or tile roofs. Essentially the houses required a door opening directly on to the road, preferably with a porch or with windows within the main building facing both ways (and these are the distinguishing features still evident today) which enabled the keeper to see who was coming and emerge quickly - especially when mail coaches approached as they had to be allowed to proceed without stopping and without payment, upon a trumpet call from the driver or guard.

Cary's Traveller's Companion or a Delineation of the Turnpike Roads of England and Wales.
This book was commissioned by the Postmaster General and was based on a survey of English and Welsh turnpike roads undertaken by John Cary and Aaron Arrowsmith from 1780. The book was first published in 1790 and in print until 1828. The page above is from the 1806 edition. The book was a great influence on the initial work of the Ordnance Survey, established in 1791.

Accommodation was limited, often on one floor only although in a few cases there was an upper room accessed via steep stairs or a ladder. Conditions for the keeper and his family would have been hard even without the animosity of local people. He had to attend his gate at all hours of the day and night. He was accountable to the Trust for whom he worked and had to be reasonably competent in simple book-keeping. The scale of charges was displayed on a board fixed to the gate or to the house, and on some of the old toll houses it's possible to recognise their former position by a blanked recess on the wall, with hinges for a lamp.

One can imagine there would have been many disputes, not to mention delays at the gates, while tolls were settled, all causing aggravation to the road users who found gates being erected all around them. Many towns had them covering every exit, making movement expensive and adding significantly to trade costs.

By 1728 an Act had been passed making the destruction of, or to, a toll gate punishable by three months in jail and a whipping. A second conviction led to transportation. However, this did little to suppress vandalism and serious riots occurred in Herefordshire and Somerset involving large numbers of people. Heavier tolls were imposed in 1741 to compensate for heavier loads and heavier vehicles, and in some places weighing machines were introduced – outside Llangollen for example. There were complaints that some Trustees were taking unfair advantage of local people and were profiteering or neglecting their duty by failing to use funds to repair and maintain roads under their jurisdiction.

Over the next hundred years the number of Turnpike Trusts grew, each one responsible for a limited area, and the mileage of turnpiked roads increased to many thousands. The Trusts had the advantage of being controlled by landowners and other influential people, but their limited powers resulted in a hotchpotch of a road system.

The man appointed Superintendent General of the Road for the county of Bristol in 1815 was John Loudon McAdam who used his position to experiment with a new system of repairing and surfacing roads in his area. In 1816 he treated a stretch of eleven miles of road between Bristol and Old Down in a special way. The experiment proved effective and three years later the surface was still in a remarkably good condition. This method was the result of great attention to correct grading and selection of materials, also great care with drainage. These were all points stressed by Thomas Telford who brought sound engineering principles to road construction. McAdam made further progress and created a waterbound dust surface created by the slow grinding motion of heavy wagon wheels, reinforced with lime to bind it. Another feature was the introduction of a sensible camber – McAdam advocated a rise of only three inches over a road width of eighteen feet. A gradient of one in thirty was considered satisfactory and used on the London to Holyhead road which Thomas Telford was asked to improve.

However, by the 1840s there was a great deal of unrest, particularly in parts of Wales, where local people took it upon themselves to confront the authorities to object to the unfair imposition of a great number of toll gates and bars. And by the end of the 19th century, with Trusts losing money because trade and traffic was moving to the railways, Parliament was persuaded to withdraw the legislation. In towns across the country there were celebrations, with people throwing open or burning gates and many toll houses were sold at auction for private residential use.

The Life and Times of a Toll House Keeper

Although the position of Toll House Keeper had to be held by someone trust-
worthy, it is probable that the work of collecting tolls would not have attracted
many people and, with its long hours, hardships and even abuse, would have
had little to offer. In his *Diary* Kilvert wrote:

*Called at the Bridge Gate House on the Merediths. Mrs Meredith told me she had seen
better days. She once kept the Monmouth Gap Hotel and a coaching establishment of
eighteen horses, sixteen of which died of 'flu at one time. Then her husband died and
she moved with her five children to the shop opposite the hotel and brought them up.
Her second husband was a small timber merchant who was ruined by the failure of a
man in the same business. Now they have come down to keep a turnpike gate.*

Charles Dickens wrote in his book *Martin Chuzzlewit:*

*The tollman - a crusty customer, always smoking solitary pipes in a Windsor chair
inside, set artfully between two little windows that looked up and down the road, so
that when he saw anything coming up he might hug himself on having toll to take, and
when he saw it going down, might hug himself on having taken it …*

There are many references to the violence experienced by toll house keepers. In the weekly newspaper *Hue and Cry* of 1818 it said:

*Daring Robbery - Joshue Bigram, the Toll-collector at the Gate at Tokely, on the Dun-
mow Road, leading to Bishops Stortford, was hailed with the usual call of persons
wanting to pass through the Toll Gate. On going out he was violently seized by four
men disguised, who forced him into the Toll House and having plundered it of the
money, amounting to between £40 and £50, and having ill-treated him fast in a
chair, they made their escape . . .*

Unless the toll house was situated immediately outside a busy town it would
have been a lonely existence for a toll-keeper on bleak, dark roads often
menaced by robbers, highwaymen and people evading payment of their fees.

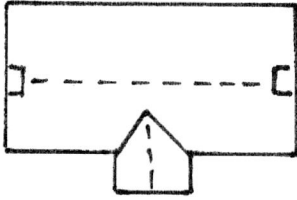

Hendre, Clwyd.

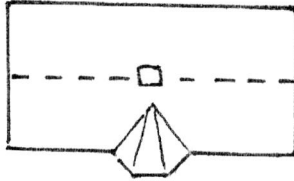

Caerwys, Clwyd.

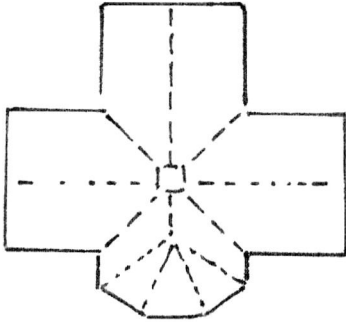

Capel Curig
4
Corwen

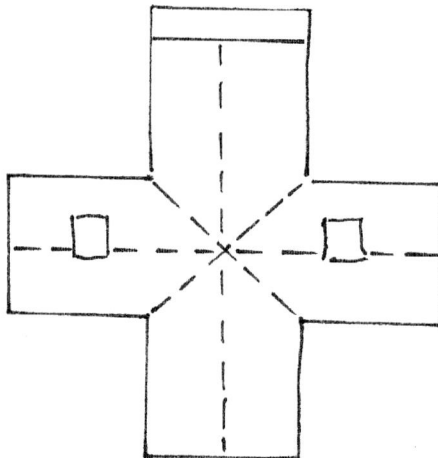

Rebecca Gate

Typical layouts
of toll houses.

In *Pickwick Papers* Charles Dickens refers to them again:

Tony Weller, turning to Mr Pickwick says:
"Wery queer life is a pike-keeper's, sir."
"A what?" Said Mr. Pickwick ...
"The old 'un means a turnpike keeper, gen'lm'n," observed Mr Samuel Weller in
explanation.
"Oh," said Mr. Pickwick, "I see. Yes; very curious life - very uncomfortable."
"They're all on 'em as has met vith some disappointment in life, consequence of vich
they retires from the world, and shuts themselves up in pikes; partly vith the view of
being solitary, and partly to rewenge themselves on mankind by taking tolls . . . If they
was gen'lm'n, you'd call 'em misanthropes, but as it is, they only turns to pike-keepin'."

In *Country Toll Gates*, 1858, by Thomas Miller, he says:

It is a solitary life to keep watch at these dreary toll gates day after day, and night after
night; places where the traffic is so small that the Tolls taken scarcely pay for keeping
the roads in repair. A horseman pulls up, pays his penny and the old man, merely
because it is a change, watches him until he is out of sight, then for hours he hears not
the sound of a human voice for no one comes that way, for there is nowhere to go to, no
place to stop at, but the market town ten miles off. But few have travelled through Eng-
land without being struck by the solitary situation of some of the Toll Gates which
they have passed through and what must their loneliness be now when such a number
of coaches have been taken off the roads. For we fancy that the sound of the horn, and
the thundering of the guard at the gate in the deep mid night were often, in those dreary
places, welcome company. But in the silent out of the way country, where three or four
long, houseless weary, lane like roads, come through woods, and between hills, and meet
at some murderous looking angle, that is the spot for a romantic and lonely Toll Gate.

Here is a letter written in 1827 to the Commissioners of the Hackwood Lane Toll Gate (probably Trustees of the Alton to Basingstoke Road):

Gentlemen,
I took the Liberty of Righting to the Commissioners of the Road in Dispute with Mrs
E. Withers. It appears that Mrs Withers has been a Toll Collector Almost this thirty
years and Having rented this Gate in Question three years before the last lease and
always collected the Tolls by a Sertain Toll Board Erected on the Toll House At the
time of taking this Last Lease Nothing was said to the Contrary that the Tolls was not
to be Taken nor was the Toll Board taken down but Suffered to Remain and Collected

by from the 13 Sept Till the 1 Day of Jany when a fresh Toll Board was put up and I Beg to Say that the Toll Board is to be found If you Gentlemen will Desire it to be Brought forward.

And I also States that the Verry Toll Board wich is fixt on the House at this Moment Is not wright According to your Act.

Mrs Withers Also Informs Me that Several Times did She Attend the Meeting Begging to be Relieved But In vain and Gentlemen I am Sorry to Inform You that owing to the Suit Being Carried on against Her She has Paid in London £178 into the Hands Of one of the Clerks of the Kings Bench and Smith of Reading as Received of her £152 Making in All the sum of £330 for this suit. It is to be understood If the Gentlemen do not take this Matter Into Consideration It as Ruined the Small Family which She as to Support which as Gentlemen I hope you Will Consider as to Fatherless Children Gentlemen

This Requires the Attention of you Gentlemen as I consider It is of A Most Serious Nature and as far as I could do I wish to See the Matter Settled if Possible there is A Large Family and the Annormous Sum It as Cost As Run away with all the Money Nearly and If Some Arrangement Shall be Made to Settle It If Possible As She always wished to Pay what was Right.

I Am Gentlemen
Your Obedient Servant George Maskel
London June 5 1827

Trade Movements

In 1835 an Essex newspaper printed the following:

Canals and turnpike roads are the arteries through which
the wealth - the life-blood - of the nation circulates.

By the early 19th century one of the main commodities being transported around the country was salt, a product used to preserve meat, as a cleansing agent and for tanning hides. 'Saltways' led away from coastal regions and from former tropical seas such as those in Cheshire, where the springs were said to be ten times saltier than ordinary sea water. (The Romans had obtained salt from these former seas near Droitwich and Middlewich by boiling the brine to evaporate the water.) Packhorses were the beasts of burden used to distribute goods all over the country and they trailed in long 'strings' with their heavy loads, led by a man called a 'jagger'. They were muzzled to prevent them from grazing as they moved along, and the leading ones wore bells to warn people of the approach of the convoy. Huge baskets with loads of about two-hundred-weight of goods were fastened to the back of each horse on a narrow saddle, and it is still possible to see a few remaining packhorse bridges which were built with very low parapets to allow the baskets adequate room to pass over the bridge without getting snagged.

The heaviness of the loads and the great number of hooves caused tremendous damage to highways and byways. As trade increased throughout the country other means of transporting goods had to be found. As long ago as 1646 a man named Thomas Pickford set up business in Cheshire where he operated a quarry, obtaining a contract to carry stones for repairing roads in and around Macclesfield. At first he used horses to carry loads in panniers, travelling in single file in gangs of forty or fifty, linked head to tail. The firm flourished and by the middle of the 18th century they were using broad-wheeled vehicles pulled by a team of six or more horses, called stage-wagons. As speed became more competitive stage-wagons were replaced by lighter, better sprung conveyances called fly-wagons, and these were able to move at a trot. They were a compromise between the lumbering stage-wagons which allowed just a few passengers on board (those too poor to travel by stage-coach), and the purely passenger stage-coaches. The firm of Pickfords remains in existence to this day.

Trade was stimulated all over the country with better transport and better roads. Flints were carried from Grimes Graves near Norwich to London and fish, preserved in local salt, from the coast. Derbyshire millstones were used throughout Britain; its lead was used extensively for cathedral roofs and was taken to Bath to make the lining and pipes for the Great Bath; hides from London were taken to Hull, along rivers to Bawtry to reach Yorkshire and Derbyshire; coal came through the Goyt Valley, and Kendal was a great meeting place for packhorse trains taking cloth, wool, malt and feathers to other regions. Wagons from Manchester regularly visited large towns like Edinburgh, Bristol, London and Birmingham, and a journey which had previously taken four and a half days took only thirty-six hours half a century later.

Riots!

Turnpikes and toll houses were not generally welcomed by locals and there were many instances of violent opposition. One mob from Yeadon and Otley demolished a dozen gates and at Selby the public bellman called the inhabitants to destroy the gates. In June 1753 a great number of rioters marched from Leeds to destroy the newly-erected turnpike gate at Harewood Bridge. A Mr Lascelles assembled a defending force of three hundred men, and thirty rioters were taken prisoner, ten of them held in York Castle. A week later the military were called to defend the district's turnpikes; three people were arrested and imprisoned and rioters attempted to free them. There was an ugly scene outside the Old Kings Arms in Briggate, Leeds, where the magistrates and turnpike trustees sat at the time. The Riot Act was read and troops opened fire. Eight people were killed, and forty wounded. After this unfortunate sequence of events matters settled down and the roads began to be improved.

In his book *Wild Wales (1862),* George Borrow wrote: 'whosoever fill the office of turnpike-keeper should be a person of very considerable nerve'. He goes on to recount a conversation with a certain John Jones with whom he was walking:

After we had left the gate I asked John Jones whether he had ever heard of Rebecca of the toll-gates.

"Oh yes," said he, "I have heard of that chieftainess."

"And who was she?" said I.

"I cannot say, sir; I never saw her, nor nay one who had seen her. Some say that there were a hundred Rebeccas, and all of the them men dressed in women's clothes, who went about at night, at the head of bands to break the gates. Ah, sir, something of the kind was almost necessary at that time. I am a friend of peace, sir; no head-breaker, housebreaker, nor gate-keeper, but I can hardly blame what was done at that time, under the name of Rebecca. You have no idea how the poor Welsh were oppressed by those gates, aye, and the rich too. The little people and farmers could not carry their produce to market owing to the exactions at the gates, which devoured all the profit and sometimes more. So that the markets were not half supplied, and people with money could

frequently not get what they wanted. Complaints were made to government, which not being attended to, Rebecca and her byddinion made their appearance at night, and broke the gates to pieces with sledge-hammers, and everyone said it was gallant work, everybody save the keepers of the gates and proprieters. Not only the poor, but the rich said so. Aye, and I have heard that many a fine young gentleman had a hand in the work, and went about at night at the head of a band dressed as Rebecca. Well sir, those breakings were acts of violence, I don't deny, but they did good, for the system is altered.

It is not difficult to understand why the Rebecca Riots erupted as they did. Tension had been growing in rural Wales since the end of the Napoleonic Wars of 1815 which depressed the economy. By 1839 conditions in West Wales were at their worst level and in some cases toll gates were destroyed time and time again, and toll houses were burnt down despite the intervention of the military who had been assembled in the area due to trouble with the Chartists. A strong religious thread, nurtured by their preachers, ran through Welsh congregations at this time, and the injustices endured began to boil over in an emotional response. The Bible was studied and memorised in minute detail and matters of concern were aired in chapels and fairs as well as lodgings where country people spent the night on journeys.

The scandalous behaviour of a man named Thomas Bullin, a greedy 'Toll-farmer' further fermented the unrest. He had holdings of many toll gates across southern England, from the East End of London to Portsmouth, around Bristol, across south Wales to Swansea and into Carmarthenshire and Pembrokeshire. He, and the Whitland Trust for whom he worked, had many gates erected at the very time farmers began to haul lime to their fields and farmers were already struggling due to the depressed livestock prices. Further north at Rhayader, Llangurig, Llandiloes, Newtown and Welshpool people were facing ruin in the flannel weaving industry due to the depression and the new steam-driven mills of north England. Farmers had been paying

10% of their annual income to the Church, and between 1836 and 1844 this rose by 7%, which further angered an already disgruntled populace.

It is thought that a man called Thomas Rees (Twm Carnabwth) became their leader and a quotation from the Bible in the Book of Genesis became their inspiration – where Rebecca was implored to become 'the mother of thousands of millions, and let thy seed possess the gates of those which hate them'. Rees was said to be a prize fighter, a drinker and a lover of excitement as well as being a reciter of the catechism at chapel, with a strong sense of morality and justice. Nocturnal rides in boisterous company were part of his life and he would have thought nothing of leading groups into the destruction of toll gates wearing women's clothes and blackened faces, all part of 'Ceffyl Pren' tradition (Welsh mob justice).

Thomas Bullin began to notice people evading toll gates on several miles of the Main Trust on the roads around Carmarthen and on its border with Brecon in the east and into Pembrokeshire in the west, on the route towards Milford Haven where ships departed for Ireland and America. With considerable bad timing Bullin ordered a gate to be set up east of St Clears crossroads, and it was the destruction of this gate in 1842 which marked the beginning of the Rebecca revolt and war on the Main, Whitland and Tavernspite Trusts.

Despite the risk of harsh sentencing if caught, the people of Wales caused such consternation in London that the legislature was moved to climb down and ease their burden, and for the next fifty years (until virtually ceasing in the 1890s) tolls played a diminishing part in the highway system.

Let it not be thought that the difficulties experienced in Wales were the only ones that arose. In Northumberland an 1843 report stated:

Rebecca in Northumberland. On Saturday last a Turnpike gate at the entrance of the village of Ponteland, about 7 miles from this town, was forcibly broken down. The gatekeeper declining to pass a party without Toll, they deliberately broke it in pieces, and passed quietly through. We do not think that this affair is the result of any organized party, but simply from the conviction that the Toll is not a legal one.

The Examiner, 1856, draws attention to the problems experienced by Londoners:

The modern City of 100 Gates is London . . . there are no less than eighty-seven Turnpike Gates and Bars within the four mile cab radius from Charing Cross. We are too conservative and moderate to call Rebecca from the Welsh Mountains but . . !

The London to Holyhead Road

The Act of Union with Ireland in 1801 made Holyhead particularly important as it was the chief port for travellers between the two countries. Ireland at this time had some 5 million inhabitants, while the population of Great Britain was only 12 million. The union with Ireland meant that Irish Members of Parliament had to travel to and from Westminster and the conditions on their journeys brought discomforts into sharp relief.

There were seventeen Turnpike Trusts between London and Shrewsbury, and seven more between Shrewsbury and Holyhead. The further west travellers went, the worse the road conditions that were experienced. In 1808 the Post Office attempted to extend the mailcoach service to Holyhead, but it failed; riding 'post' was so dangerous that in one week three post horses fell and broke legs. It could take thirteen hours to cross Anglesey by mailcoach on the old road, which was no more than twelve feet wide and passed along the edge of unprotected precipices. Reynardson's *Reminiscenses of a Gentleman Coachman* includes the following reference to the road:

The pace of the Chester Mail to Holyhead of nine and a half miles per hour, including stoppage was, I used to think, quite fast enough for a night mail. The road, generally speaking, was rather narrow and in many places full of twists and turns, with some sharpish hills, and on a dark night in winter you were obliged to keep your eyes well about you or, rather, in front of you. Our Friend in Red behind had in many places to 'keep his horn going' pretty often to warn the sleepy Welshman that the Toll Gates must be open.

In 1810 the government employed Thomas Telford to propose improvements to the Shrewsbury to Holyhead road but reconstruction didn't actually
begin until the Irish MP Sir Henry Parnell took up the cause in 1815; work
on the road continued for a further fifteen years thereafter. The overall design
and specification for Telford's road made it safer and easier for horse-drawn
coaches, eliminating steep hills and sharp corners. His re-alignments on Anglesey replaced the circuitous turnpike with a direct and graded route to the
harbour at Holyhead. Telford's technique, perfected in his work in Scotland,
was more expensive than that employed by John McAdam, a contemporary,
but the fact that much of this road remains today is evidence of his great skill.

Telford's engineering feats made it possible to reduce the number of turnpike trusts on the Shrewsbury to Holyhead road from twenty-three to five,
and a few of these toll houses still survive, as well as the milestones.

The whole length of the road from Shrewsbury to Holyhead was supplied
with new milestones which cost £5 each to install and weighed 23 cwt each,
quarried from fine, hard limestone, a type of marble found near Red Wharf
Bay on the coast of Anglesey. Telford also designed gates, some in a 'rising sun'
pattern, in wrought iron. The bridge which spans the hazardous waters of the
Menai Straits further exemplifies his incredible career and is, perhaps, a fitting
monument to his skill. Only recently has his bridge been superseded.

From the early 19th century it became increasingly common to bolt metal
plates on to milestones with details cast in relief. Others were of cast iron
with place names on two faces, often with the distance from London. There
are some very interesting designs in existence all over the country, worthy of
preservation.

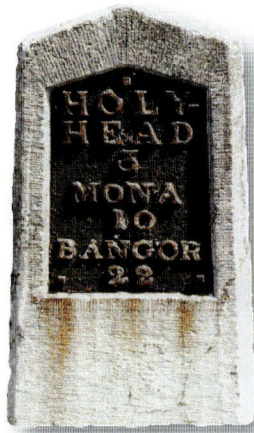

Sir Henry Parnell wrote that tolls often increased when good toll houses were provided, and Telford designed fifteen toll houses to a standard pattern, mostly four-roomed bungalows with projecting bays (such as the one shown on page 84, at Blists Hill Museum) on the mainland, and two-storey houses on Anglesey. In his *Treatise on Road*, Sir Henry Parnell cited the 'Specification for Building Telford's toll house at Llanfair, in the Island of Anglesey', as follows:

The toll house is to be built at the precise spot now marked out on the ground, and to be in shape and dimensions to the above drawings.

The masonry to be of good sound rubble-work, except the plinth, steps and sills, which are to be of good hammer-dressed freestone, or slate. The whole to be set in good lime and sand mortar.

The sills of the door and window frames to be of oak; the rest of the frames, and outer woodwork, to be of Baltic fir, except the posts of the portico, which are to be of sound round oak. All inside timber-work to be of Baltic fir.

The roof to be covered with slates, and the hips, ridges, and gutters to be covered with lead eighteen inches wide, and not less than seven pounds to the square foot.

The inside wall and ceilings to be plastered three coats, and set. The under side of the portico, and the projection of roof, to be also ceiled and plastered, and faced with a three-and-a-half inch fascia board. The outside to be roughcast and coloured.

The portico to be paved with pebble, with a hammer-dressed plinth, for the posts to stand upon, at least twelve inches wide. The octagonal lower room and the wash-house to be paved with tiles.

All woodwork to be painted three times in oil; the inside works finished white, with doors and skirting oak colour, and the outside work dark green.

There are to be proper grates, with slate chimney-pieces, to all rooms.

A garden is to be fenced round on three sides, each of twenty yards, with a walk of the same description as those on each side of the new road.

In this garden a privy is to be built, with proper roof, dome, seat, etc. complete.

There are to be two wrought-iron toll gates, one across the road to Plas-newydd, and the other across that to Holyhead. There are also to be two turnstiles, and posts and rails to be of sound oak; to be painted three times in oil, white. The contractor to find all the materials and labour.

Who Goes There? - Your Money or Your Life!

Georgian England, often considered to be the epitome of glamour and elegance, was in fact crime ridden and violent. Crowds, sometimes led by women, would use force to stop dealers selling corn above fixed prices, and bread and food riots were common. At one time Norwich suffered for several days when mobs objected to the price of mackerel. Turnpike riots took place in Gloucestershire, Nottingham and Yorkshire, and a number of the rioters were killed.

The terrible state of the roads was not the only hazard to be faced in the early days of travel when all manner of men became 'Gentlemen of the Road'. Soldiers returning from the Civil War who could not find employment were desperate sometimes for money; sons of the aristocracy who had run up large debts at gaming tables took to the road to replenish their pockets; well-educated men seeking a glamorous life-style found it a thrill to terrorise travellers, and others who were the real rogues simply wanted to accumulate lots of money and did not care how they got it. Some were Royalists who claimed they robbed only followers of Oliver Cromwell. Anyone intending to travel was well advised to hide money and jewellery beneath their clothing and many considered it almost inevitable they would be robbed once on a journey, sometimes more frequently. One of the worst places in Yorkshire for highwaymen and footpads was the Calder Valley, in the narrow pass between Todmorden and Hebden Bridge where steep, dark cliffs offered shelter for robbers to descend at great speed on their victims.

Before the establishment of banks, wealthy landowners and merchants, as well as royalty and courtiers, carried large sums of money on their persons making easy targets for robbers unless they were accompanied by servants or were armed. London, with its many narrow lanes crowded with people from all over the country, provided thieves with plenty of hiding places but if caught they were imprisoned and many were hanged on gallows at Tyburn. It is said that on one road leading out of Shoreditch the turnpike men were issued with speaking trumpets through which they were instructed to shout warnings to people travelling through of the danger or proximity of highwaymen and apparently this was quite effective. At Kensington a bell was rung at intervals on Sunday evenings to muster a group of would-be passengers to travel together for safety. The Sunday Trading Act of 1676 made sure that anyone foolish enough to travel in the hours of darkness or on Sunday must be prepared to suffer the consequences, and during these excluded periods the Hundred (the area where the robbery had been committed) was not responsible for repayment of their losses. A highwayman was known to haunt the Knightsbridge area where he would rob coaches that stuck in the mud where a stream from Hyde Park ran across the road. In the 1780s nearly a hundred criminals were hanged annually in London and Middlesex at Tyburn (now known as Marble Arch) – the usual penalty for convicted robbers until the punishment was replaced by transportation. A toll house stood on the former site of the permanent gallows from about 1760 to 1829 and a stone gatepost from one of the three toll gates is set in the window of a bank in Edgware Road, with a commemorative plaque.

Journeys northward along the Great North Road, and south to Dover, westward to Windsor where the Court was held, were targeted by highwaymen, as was the road to Bath where wealthy people went to bathe in the mineral waters. Salisbury Plain was a hazardous area, as were many of the commons and forests.

Alconbury Hill was the threshold of a robbing place that came close in notoriety to Gads Hill near Rochester, Hounslow Heath and Finchley Common. It was called Stonegate Hole, between the 64th and 65th milestones from London. In a deep, solitary hollow at the foot of a northward slope, it was shut in by dense woods. In the later coaching era when the road was lowered and earth filled into the hollow, many bones were found – supposed relics of unfortunate travellers who had met their death by highwaymen.

Names such as Claude Duval and Dick Turpin, even to this day, are evocative of an era that may seem thrilling and glamorous but in fact was dangerous and unenviable. In a move to reduce robberies, John Palmer of Bath persuaded the government in 1784 to transfer the mail from horse-riding boys to stage coaches. Mail coaches were allowed to pass through toll gates without stopping and without payment of tolls. Strict schedules were kept and the toll keeper was warned of the approach by the driver or guard sounding a horn. Improved road conditions and better vehicles gradually led to faster journey times; the London to Holyhead journey was reduced from forty-four hours fifty minutes to twenty-six hours fifty-five minutes, an average speed of ten miles an hour.

Mail Guards were instructed by the Post Master General in 1830 thus:

On no account to give up his station to another person. He is to take care that his firearms are kept in clean and good condition, always properly loaded and primed when

on duty and on no account whatever is he to discharge his blunderbuss or pistol as the carriage is going along the Turnpike Road or through a town. He is to sound his horn as a signal for carriages to turn out of the way upon the approach of the Mail Coach also to warn the Turnpike men of his coming that no unnecessary delay may be occasioned and likewise to prepare postmasters against its arrival and Horsekeepers to bring out their horses at each of the changing places, and he is to sound it always as a signal to passengers when the time is expired that is allowed in the Time Bill for their stopping to refresh, and use his utmost exertions to prevent delay in all cases whatever.

An amusing incident is recorded in *Bell's Life in London & Liverpool Sporting Register* of 1826:

The Mail Horn. A country postmaster who is in the habit of rising every night to deliver the bag with its letters to the mail coach as it passes through the town in which he lives, made a very ludicrous mistake. Hearing the sound of the horn, he started from his sleep, opened the window and threw out the bag as he thought, to the guard who deposited what he had received in the proper place. At the next stage on the turnpike road to London it was discovered that instead of the bag the postmaster had thrown his breeches into the coach. The postmaster soon perceived the blunder he had committed, set off with the bag and, overtaking the coach, recovered his small clothes!

And What of the Future?

By the middle of the 19th century speed in communication had become increasingly important and railways were thriving. The demise of toll keepers and toll collection rapidly followed.

In 1859 Charles Dickens wrote in *The Uncommercial Traveller*:

I came to the Turnpike and found it, in its silent way, eloquent respecting the change that had fallen on the road. The Turnpike-house was all overgrown with ivy; and the Turnpike keeper unable to get a living out of the tolls, plied the trade of a cobbler. Not only that, but his wife sold ginger-beer and, in the very window of espial through which the Toll-takers of old times used with awe to behold the grand London coaches coming on at a gallop, exhibited for sale little barber's poles of sweetstuff in a sticky lantern. The political economy of the master of the turnpike thus expressed itself.

"How goes turnpike business, master?" Said I to him, as he sat in his little porch repairing a shoe.

"It don't go at all, master," said he to me. "It's stopped."

"That's bad," said I.

"Bad?" he repeated. And he pointed to one of his sunburnt dusty children who was climbing the turnpike gate, and said, extending his open right hand in remonstrance with Universal Nature, "Five on 'em!"

"But how to improve Turnpike business?" said I.

"There's a way, master," said he, with the air of one who had thought deeply on the subject.

"I should like to know it."

"Lay a toll on everything as comes through; lay a toll on walkers. Lay another toll on everything as don't come through; lay a toll on them as stops at home."

"Would the last remedy be fair?"

"Fair? Them as stops at home could come through if they liked, couldn't they?"

"Say they could."

"Toll 'em. If they don't come through it's their look out. Anyway - Toll 'em!"

Finding it was impossible to argue with this financial genius as if he had been Chancellor of the Exchequer and consequently the right man in the right place, I passed on meekly.

By the end of the century a fascinating and sometimes difficult era of history had passed and speed was increasingly of the essence.

Today measures are sought to divert traffic away from heavily congested areas with by-passes and new toll roads. Solutions are sought by government to pay for increased road maintenance due to unimaginably heavy lorries and vast numbers of private vehicles. The creation of new toll roads has been suggested many times and recently an article in the *Daily Telegraph* newspaper commented, 'Tolls are not wrong in principle. Those who use a service must pay for it, and tolls have a role in the funding of a road network . . . Revenue should be spent on improving the roads . . . Our economy is hugely dependent on the car and on road transport.'

Perhaps use could be made of some of the existing small houses jutting on to and overlooking turnpike roads throughout England and Wales? They would certainly be more attractive than modern toll booths!

The horn that once upon the mail
Its soul of music shed,
Now hangs all mute against the wall,
And tells of guards long dead;
So sleeps the horn of former years,
Its stirring sounds are o'er,
And toll bar men and horsekeepers
Now hear that sound no more.

Toll Houses in England

Tidmarsh, Berkshire

1812 - GRADE II LISTED
TOLL HOUSE NATIONAL ID BE.TID

To the west of Reading, linking the Bristol road to the (private) toll bridge over the Thames at Pangbourne, the road runs through the village of Tidmarsh. Originally this was a narrow, twisting lane close to the mansion of a large estate until it was straightened due to an exchange of lands, thus permitting it to be taken away from the large house. The road was turnpiked and this neat house was erected.

The space for the toll board can be clearly seen, but the 'spy' windows to the porch are screened by a hedge.

High Wycombe, Buckinghamshire
1841 - GRADE II LISTED
TOLL HOUSE NATIONAL ID BU.HWY

Built in 1826 on the London to Oxford road this toll house became derelict and was rescued and rebuilt between 1982 and 1991 for the Chiltern Open Air Museum, Chalfont St Giles, Buckinghamshire. Records show it was built originally for about £500 and although it is very small it was occupied by a family of five in 1841. In its new setting it looks most attractive, with its slate roof, castellated walls and a small clock over the doorway, on a gated roadway.

Macclesfield, Cheshire

1780 - GRADE II LISTED
TOLL HOUSE NATIONAL ID CH.SUT

The dried up remains of a former tropical sea have been excavated for many centuries in Cheshire. Brine from natural springs was boiled to evaporate the water. The *Domesday Book* details tolls on the transport of salt by carts pulled by oxen or horses. So important was the trade in salt that numerous place names were given to features of the saltways or the fields where the horses grazed or rested, such as 'Salterslane', 'Saltersfield' or 'Saltersbrook'. The bridges over which the packhorses passed were built with low parapets to give room for the panniers to pass.

This cottage at Sutton Lane Ends stands on the main road skirting the edge of the Peak District which became the principal route south to London out of Manchester in the latter part of the 18th century. Its exterior has been treated in an unusual fashion. Considering the importance of the turnpike road it is surprising a more imposing house was not erected.

A nearby toll house was at Flash, in a neighbourhood that had a reputation for unlicensed traders. They obtained their goods in Macclesfield and hawked them around the country, selling buttons, laces and other trifles, taking opportunities to steal en route. Their activities gave rise to the description of someone or something as 'flashy' - cheap but showy.

Callington (Newbridge) Cornwall

1874 - GRADE II LISTED
TOLL HOUSE NATIONAL ID C.W.CAL01

The mining of copper helped build up a thriving industry in this region of Cornwall in the 19th century and nearby Kit Hill has been described as 'a treasure house of industrial archaeology'. Increasing population and burgeoning trade made improvement of roads necessary. River valleys cutting through the moorland gave rise to steep, winding roads with bridges that were difficult for horse-drawn vehicles to negotiate. From this toll house at Callington Bridge it was customary for the keeper to have a supply of extra horses to assist in the climbing of the hill as far as a roadside stone on which was inscribed 'Take Off', where the extra horse would be unhitched.

Turnpike Cottage, pictured here, is believed to date from the beginning of the 19th century, but the bridge shows two dates: '1692' at the base, and '1874' on the parapet, which would be around the time when the Turnpike Trust ended and the County Council's responsibility commenced.

Devoran, Feock, Cornwall

MID 19TH CENTURY - GRADE II LISTED
TOLL HOUSE NATIONAL ID C.W.FEO 01

Truro grew as an inland seaport in the Middle Ages and became a prosperous market town. It was also at the centre of the tin mining area from the 14th century and became a 'stannary' town - an official centre for the testing of tin and copper prior to being coined and sold. Turnpike roads converged on the cathedral city which rapidly became the commercial heart of Cornwall in the 19th century. Later the railway reinforced this but, in turn, brought about the downfall of the turnpikes.

Elegant Georgian residences were built for the wealthy businessmen, but this tiny toll house in Devoran on the main road to Truro is not in the same league despite a certain stylish use of materials.

Daniel Defoe said of Truro:

. . . the trade is now in a manner wholly gone to Falmouth, the trade at Truro being now, chiefly if not only, for shipping off of block TINN and copper ore, the latter being lately found in large quantities in some of the mountains between Truro and St Michaels . . . This is the particular town where the lord warden of the Stanneries always holds his famous Parliament of Miners, and for stamping of TINN.

Gunnislake, Cornwall

1772 - NOT GRADED
TOLL HOUSE NATIONAL ID DV.GUL01

On the road from Tavistock to Liskeard, the original turnpike descended directly down the steep hillside to the bridge crossing. Later it was diverted in zig-zag manner to give an easier gradient. When the road was altered the view from the windows would have been obscured in this curious design.

The graceful seven-arched bridge was built c.1520 and was the lowest crossing point of the Tamar river until modern times. During the Civil War it was defended by Royalists. This was an important mining area (several old chimneys remain) and minerals were exported down the river.

Casterton, Cumbria

MID TO LATE 18TH CENTURY - GRADE II LISTED
TOLL HOUSE NATIONAL ID CB.CAS

The little village of Casterton has connections with Henry VIII who, at some time, stayed in a nearby manor house which is said to be haunted by the ghost of Anne Boleyn. It also has links with the Brontes who were pupils at the Clergy Daughters' School.

Casterton lies on the line of a Roman road following the Lune valley and has a name suggesting Roman origins; it would have connected Sedbergh with Lancaster. Nearby Kendal was the centre of the woollen trade and in the 1770s became very important for the economy of the region.

This toll house, with its unusual bowed front, would have played an important role in collecting tolls from passing carts and wagons in an area that became a great centre for the turnpike network. Nearby lies Kirkby Lonsdale with its famous ancient bridge.

Grasmere, Cumbria

19TH CENTURY - NOT GRADED
TOLL HOUSE NATIONAL ID CB.LAK

This cottage, on the busy road leading north out of Grasmere, looks like an ordinary farmhouse. With interesting stepped gable ends it functioned as a toll house on the turnpike road leading to Keswick. In more recent times the carriageway was re-aligned away from the building to give an easier gradient up the long hill.

Further down the road there is an old coaching inn named The Traveller's Rest with a sign depicting a stagecoach. No doubt the horses (and passengers) would have been glad to stop for a rest in this wild moorland area when the tracks were in a wretched condition.

In the late 1700s a coach journey north of here from Carlisle to London took three days, and inside passengers paid a fare of £3.16s, outside passengers paid £2.6s.

Today, in addition to the attraction of beautiful hills and lakes, this region is popular with tourists and walkers and known for its association with the poet William Wordsworth who lived in Grasmere at Dove Cottage.

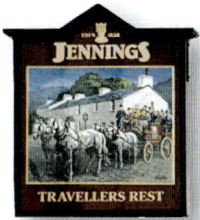

Keswick, Cumbria

19TH CENTURY - GRADE II LISTED
TOLL HOUSE NATIONAL ID KES02

The name 'Keswick' means cheese farm, and the rural economy was based on a variety of farm products (wool and leather) until the discovery of black lead at Seathwaite in Borrowdale in the 16th century which led to the manufacture of pencils.

Mining was also important and coal, iron ore, lead, copper and graphite were transported to the coast, transforming coastal fishing villages into thriving ports. Another activity that contributed to the economy in this beautiful area of lakes and glaciated valleys was tourism, inspired by literary associations with Southey, Wordsworth and Coleridge.

Several turnpike roads were made in the 1700s. Military as well as economic reasons were responsible for the building of the Shap Turnpike. Bonnie Prince Charles travelled that way in 1745 and both his army, and the English following his retreat, had great difficulty in negotiating the old road. The old packhorse track from Kendal to Ulverstone and Kirby Ireleth was turnpiked, and a direct route from Carlisle to Keswick via Skillbeck completed the 'turnpike mania' in the Lake District. Some roads were substantially improved later when they were re-aligned and new sections were built to ease gradients. Substantial lengths of the Shap route were rebuilt to plans by McAdam.

In addition to 'Toll Bar Cottage' on Chestnut Hill, shown here, there are another two toll houses in Keswick.

Underbarrow, Cumbria

19TH CENTURY - GRADE II LISTED
TOLL HOUSE NATIONAL ID CB.UND

Until the 18th century most roads in this part of the country had not been-surfaced or engineered. The first turnpikes were four roads converging on Whitehaven, created by the town's Harbour Act of 1739. By 1753 there had been six more turnpike Acts in Cumbria that included roads from Penrith to Chalk Beck, Workington to Cockermouth, and the road over Shap.

In the central fells the Kendal to Ulverstone turnpike was authorised in 1763, having formerly been a packhorse route. This little old toll house affords relatively humble accommodation and is on a narrow lane in very undulating countryside. Notice the very simple porch with spy holes to watch for approaching traffic, in addition to a side window. It would be easy for it to pass unnoticed as it has been bypassed by improved routes in the 19th and 20th century, yet it would once have played an important role in the Lake District communication system.

Grindleford Bridge, Derbyshire

17TH CENTURY - GRADE II LISTED
TOLL HOUSE NATIONAL ID   DE.GR1

Situated on the Sheffield to Buxton Turnpike, this is an adapted 17th century house. It has a small curved bay for sightings and stands beside an old stone bridge over the Derwent river in a deep valley and at the foot of an ancient routeway, known as the 'Sir William Hill' road, that involved a very steep climb over the moors. Around 1800 the road was re-routed to run through the village of Eyam, earlier associated with the Great Plague.

'Grindleford' could mean a ford for wagons, paved with grindle stones for foot traffic.

Whatstandwell, Derbyshire

19TH CENTURY - NOT GRADED
TOLL HOUSE NATIONAL ID - NOT LISTED

Before the advent of railways it was not possible to transport milk any distance from the farms where it was produced, so farmers in rich districts converted it into cheese. In 1730 London received five hundred tons of cheese from Derbyshire, Warwickshire, Leicestershire and Staffordshire.

With the advent of new industrial processes it became important to improve communications, not least after the opening of cotton mills by Arkwright and others in the valleys around Wirksworth, a few miles distant from this former toll house. This house (formerly the Bull's Head and now the Derwent Hotel) guarded a bridge over the Derwent where the road from Mansfield met the Derby to Manchester route, and lay on a sharp bend in a deep valley overlooked by high hills.

Nearby Matlock was developed as a spa town from 1700, and more recently the local limestone scenery with its caves, wells and underground streams has become a great attraction to visitors. A flourishing transport museum is located at Chrich.

Early in the 19th century a former private road from Derby to Mat-lock was greatly improved by a turnpike road running alongside the river and this now forms the A6.

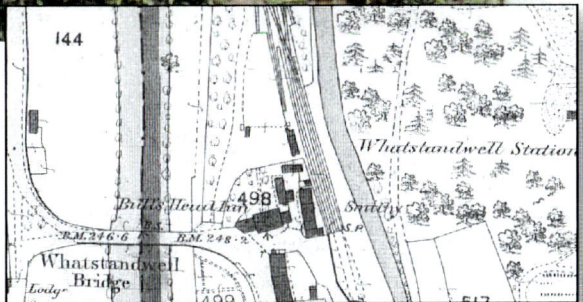

Honiton, Devon

LATE 18TH CENTURY - GRADE II LISTED
TOLL HOUSE NATIONAL ID DV.HON01

The wool trade was a major industry in Honiton from the 13th century until mills burgeoned in Yorkshire in the 18th century. The making of a special type of lace gave rise to a flourishing trade in the 17th century. The lace was very expensive and highly sought-after, and the industry employed more than 1200 workers.

Daniel Defoe, looking from the Otter Valley to the glories of Dartmoor and Exmoor, referred to the Honiton area of Devon as 'the most beautiful landscape in the world'. A series of fires destroyed much of the town in the 1700s, and now many of the buildings date from the 18th century.

The 'Copper Castle Toll House' as it is called (named after the copper penny tolls), is situated at the foot of a steep hill leading into Honiton and beside it stands a pair of very ornate gates – these may be the last remaining gates in the country left in situ. The house is one of the most fanciful to be found and has been painted in pink. There are other toll houses in the area but this is the finest.

A day of rejoicing was held when the toll gates were removed from every road in the town in 1910, but public subscription ensured the survival of the Copper Castle Toll House, and its gates, as seen today.

51

Sidmouth, Devon

1817 - GRADE II LISTED
TOLL HOUSE NATIONAL ID DV.SID01

In the 19th century Sidmouth was a favourite seaside resort, in particular for elderly and convalescent visitors, and this is reflected in the elegant and even fanciful architecture of the town.

With four pillars jutting on to the roadway, the Byes Toll House gives an imposing appearance to the eastern entrance to Sidmouth. It was built in the early 19th century and still retains the original patterned gate alongside. Note also the tall, rounded chimneys. A blue plaque on the wall indicates that the Sid Vale Association is interested in its preservation.

Yealmbridge, Devon
CIRCA 1823 - GRADE II LISTED
TOLL HOUSE NATIONAL ID DVYEA01

This attractive house has survived to the present day despite being situated on a busy road and having the usual somewhat cramped accommodation. The stonework has been whitewashed and, of course, the front door opens immediately on to the road. Built by the Modbury Turnpike Trust around 1823, it is Grade II listed and stands on the road from Plymouth to Kingsbridge. The gothic-style windows and board give it a stylish appearance but like so many toll houses it is briefly admired and then quickly forgotten in the rush to arrive at a destination.

Sherborne Hill, Dorset

19TH CENTURY - GRADE II LISTED
TOLL HOUSE NATIONAL ID DO.NOR

Elaborate, stone mullioned windows and a fine recessed porch make this an attractive house, yet by modern standards it is situated dangerously close to a very busy road junction on the A352. Not surprisingly access is now gained from the rear of the building but the windows on each side of the door still give a good view of approaching traffic.

Sherborne was a cathedral city from 705 to 1075 and now has two castles, the grounds of which Capability Brown was involved in designing in the 18th century. The town has long-established educational and religious institutions and has been famous for its silk industry. This toll house appears in Thomas Hardy novels as Sherton Turnpike.

Stanhope in Weardale, Durham

NOT GRADED
TOLL HOUSE NATIONAL ID DU.STA

This sparsely populated area near Durham and Bishop Auckland is rich in beauty-spots and was once a hunting area for mediaeval knights. It is in the heart of moorland and fells where there was once widespread mining for lead. This area was remote from the coast and the mines were dependent on organised packhorse trains to transport lead to Newcastle, and to import food for the mining population. Today, with the disappearance of the traditional industries of the North East, there has been a move to preserve the symbols of our social and economic heritage, and much of this has been brought together in the Beamish North of England Open Air Museum, towards Newcastle upon Tyne.

No doubt, in times past, this former toll house would have been the stopping-place for many a wagon en route to market.

Shenfield, Essex

18TH CENTURY - GRADE II LISTED
TOLL HOUSE NATIONAL ID EX.BRE

This very small cottage is sandwiched between more modern development in a suburban location and may seem insignificant by today's standards. It was probably not built as a toll house and may have been taken over by the Trust in the early 18th century because it lay at the junction of two important roads: on the Great Essex Road from London to Harwich, where the Essex and Middlesex Turnpikes met. It seems that this toll house brought in substantial funds for the Trust in the heyday of travel by road. An extract from *Bell's Life in London*, September 1833, refers to the Romford Turnpike, a few miles distant from this spot:

The very exorbitant and oppressive nature of the tolls on these roads has for a long time been the subject of general complaint. The inhabitants and persons trading to Romford feel the oppressions most, and have prepared a memorial, setting forth the grievances, which they intend to present to the trustees at their annual meeting which will shortly take place. The grievances of which they complain are briefly:

That the trading inhabitants of Romford pay more by way of Toll than the gentry.

Vehicles with springs paying three halfpence less than those without.

That the Toll-gates are so placed that the inhabitants of Romford cannot move out without being obliged to pay toll for the whole twenty miles of road.

The memorialists consider this as gross injustice; the principle of charge for Tolls ought, in their opinion, to be in proportion to the wear and tear occasioned.

Acton Turville, Gloucestershire

19TH CENTURY - GRADE II LISTED
TOLL HOUSE NATIONAL ID GL.ACT

Just off the M4 motorway and close to where the Badminton Horse Trials are held, this neat half-octagon, stone-dressed toll house stands on a minor road. It is difficult to understand why it was needed and why there is a second toll house within a short distance, although of a different design. The somewhat sharply pointed roof has heavy stone slates and the space where toll charges would have been displayed has been replaced with a clock.

Marshfield, Gloucestershire

19TH CENTURY - GRADE II LISTED
TOLL HOUSE NATIONAL ID GL.MAR01

Queen Anne and Georgian houses line the main street of this village which was once the last staging post for coaches from London carrying nobility and gentry to fashionable Bath. Marshfield achieved fame for making bonnets, and there are picturesque almshouses built by Elias Cope, an alderman of the City of London in the early 17th century. The main street is now very quiet, but evidence of its earlier importance lies in the coaching inns.

This toll house, thought to have been built for the Marshfield Turnpike Trust in the 19th century, is a low building with an arched porch and gothic-shaped windows and is located at the west end of the village.

Moreton-in-Marsh, Gloucestershire

19TH CENTURY
GRADE II LISTED
TOLL HOUSE NATIONAL ID   GL.MOR01

Looking like a miniature manor house with its twin gabled dormers and matching porch, this house stands at the head of the broad main street on the old Fosse Way. It is adjacent to the bridge carrying the railway which would have been responsible for its demise - ironically, trains no longer stop at the station.

After the Dissolution of the Monasteries the masons had to find employment, and the Cotswold stone was found to be easy to work, and hardened on exposure. It was used for much of the housing in the area.

Stroud, Gloucestershire (Butterrow)

1825 - GRADE II LISTED
TOLL HOUSE NATIONAL ID   GL.ROD1

Wool, and the manufacture of cloth, made the Cotswolds rich and famous in the Middle Ages. Vast flocks of sheep roaming over the hills in this region provided the resource for a major industry, which dominated the economy for several centuries. The wool and cloth merchants became very wealthy and some of them endowed the 'wool' churches which grace the landscape to this day. Fleeces were distributed to spinners and weavers in their homes, and then the woven wool would be taken to the fulling mills where it was churned around in a soapy liquid to felt the fibres together, and this made the cloth stronger and warmer. Stroud was one of the main centres for the industry, especially when Fuller's Earth was discovered there. The steep-sided valleys were particularly suited for the water mills.

This fine example of a toll house at Butterrow, Stroud, was built c.1825 at the southern edge of the town. The Trust which had it built seem to have spared no expense in its construction, with its double windows and detailing over the apertures. It has a fine board of charges.

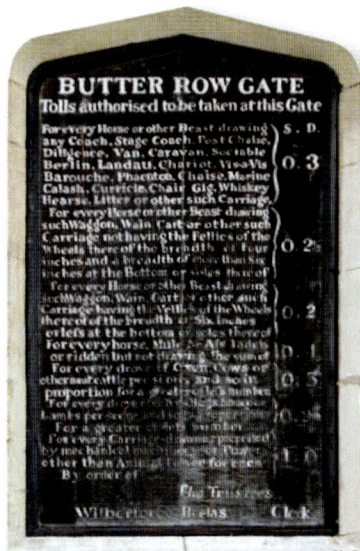

Photograph courtesy of David Gruar (creative commons.org)

Tewkesbury, Gloucestershire (Mythe Bridge)

1826 - GRADE II LISTED
TOLL HOUSE NATIONAL ID   GL.TEW01

Thomas Telford, engineer, was said to be responsible for this unusual design, with its six pinnacle pillars rising above the eaves, a pedimented roof over the porch and squint windows from which to watch any approaching traffic. It was built in conjunction with the adjacent bridge over the Severn river.

On the opposite side of the road is a booth that was probably built at the same time, with a similar door, squint windows and a bracket for a lamp or sign.

In nearby Tewkesbury, among its many interesting old buildings, there are surviving toll houses at its former southern and eastern exits.

Wotton-under-Edge, Gloucestershire

1825 - GRADE II LISTED
TOLL HOUSE NATIONAL ID   GL.WOO

The rampant, invasive climber that coats the walls and castellated roof of this toll house gives a mysterious appearance to this relic of a former prosperous business. It stands at the junction of two roads and once guarded the approach to an ancient market town where wool was traded for the cloth industry. The surrounding steep, wooded landscape was mainly farmed for sheep, and much of the land was owned by the Berkeley family who lived in nearby Berkeley Castle. At one time this was a thriving industrial area with fifteen fulling mills within five miles.

Alresford, Hampshire

19TH CENTURY - GRADE II LISTED
TOLL HOUSE NATIONAL ID   HA.NEW

Erected when the Winchester to Alton road was turnpiked in the middle of the 18th century, this house was designed with classical features, including a fine cornice and a porch jutting on to the busy road. Alresford has since been bypassed thus helping to preserve its characterful main street.

In the 12th century there was an attempt to make the river Itchen navigable from Southampton to Bishops Sutton, a short distance from Alresford; now Alresford Pond is the only remaining evidence of this effort. Before William the Conqueror, Alresford belonged to the Bishops of Winchester. Winchester was then the 'capital' of England, remaining so even after the Conquest. It is the burial place of writers Izaac Walton and Jane Austen as well as St Swithin!

Botley, Hampshire

CIRCA 1840
GRADE II LISTED
TOLL HOUSE NATIONAL ID HA.BOT

William Cobbett, journalist and farmer wrote a book called *Rural Rides* in which he expressed his concern for the country following land enclosure and the effect of the industrial revolution. Although some of his work was politically radical and seen as controversial at the time, the observations in *Rural Rides* give a fascinating insight into rural life in the early 1800s, as shown in the extract below:

Here we found a parcel of labourers at parish work . . . The harvest was over early. The hop-picking is now over; and now they are employed by the parish; that is to say, not absolutely digging holes one day and filling them up the next; but at the expense of half-ruined farmers and tradesmen and landlords, to break stones into very small pieces to make nice smooth roads lest the jolting, in going along them, should create bile in the stomach of the over-fed tax-eaters . . .

Cobbett said of Botley that 'it is the most delightful village in the world' and he actually settled there to farm. He was tried for sedition in 1830 at the time when there was a great uprising of agricultural labourers, and his subsequent acquittal made him a champion of the workers.

Botley was a small port on the river Hamble, trading in corn and timber, and its flour mill was listed in the *Domesday Book*. There was a busy market in the village and fourteen coaching inns. The Olde Gate House, quietly situated now, would have seen much activity and would have been an important post for collecting tolls.

Romsey, Hampshire

CIRCA 1860 - GRADE II LISTED
TOLL HOUSE NATIONAL ID HA.ROM

Despite its proximity to a busy roundabout close to the centre of a small town near Southampton, this toll house has been well preserved. The typical roof shape and central chimney indicate its former use, as do the windows for watching out for passers-by.

Among the pleasing old buildings in the town there is the fine Norman Abbey, with even older foundations. More recent fame has come from association with Lord Palmerston who came to live nearby at Broadlands, as did Lord Mountbatten of Burma.

Mortimers Cross, Herefordshire

NOT GRADED
TOLL HOUSE NATIONAL ID - NOT LISTED

Quite a humble toll house, rapidly passed by on a quiet road and gently concealed by its hedge, it still reflects some of the standard requirements with its angled windows for watching the road and a porch where the toll keeper could shelter from the elements when he exacted his dues.

It is difficult to imagine now that one of the bloody battles of the Wars of the Roses was fought nearby in 1460. It was here that a large army of Yorkists, led by Edward, Earl of March (son of Richard of York), confronted the Lancastrian supporters of Henry VI. Four thousand men died in the battle but the Yorkists, perhaps spurred on by Edward's sighting of three suns in the sky on the morning of the battle (a scientific phenomena known as a parhelion) were the victors and Edward marched on to London, where he was crowned King Edward IV.

Pluckley, Kent

19TH CENTURY - GRADE II LISTED
TOLL HOUSE NATIONAL ID KE.PLU

An ancient Saxon forest used to cover most of Kent, and Pluckley is situated on the Greensand Ridge in what was known as Plucca's Clearing. Weaving became one of the major cottage industries of the town, relying on local wool and fulling mills, but this collapsed when labour became cheaper in the north of England.

In the 14th century the 'Black Death' wiped out much of the population of Kent and changed the relationship between peasant and their lords, giving the peasants more freedom than they had previously enjoyed because of the demand for their labour. When the government tried to curb these freedoms with new poll taxes the peasants retaliated. In 1381 Wat Tyler, led the peasants of Kent to Canterbury, sacked the Archbishop's Palace, marched through Maidstone where they freed John Bull from prison, went to London where they seized the Tower of London, murdered the Archbishop of Canterbury and finally forced a meeting with King Richard II.

In 1766 the Biddenden to Boundgate Trust was set up to improve the poor roads across the Weald and up a steep hill through Pluckley. A toll gate was set up, probably using an existing house for the collector. The toll house pictured below, standing at a crossroads, dates back to around 1590 and at one time must have been two cottages. Also shown, opposite, is a drawing of the house as it looked a couple of hundred years ago. Brickworks, making between sixty and seventy different kinds of bricks, were a flourishing local business and many of the houses in the area are similar, with an almost uniform design of window. It is said that one of the Dering family, who have been linked with the village for centuries, escaped through such a window to avoid Round-heads, and this design has been preserved since.

The village of Pluckley has a reputation for being haunted and the Black Horse Public House especially so, despite its relocation since the first occurrence!

Barrowford, Lancashire

1805 - GRADE II LISTED
TOLL HOUSE NATIONAL ID LA.BAR01

From 1542 there was a large mill here which ground corn for all the farms in the area, and later there was a fulling mill which was converted into a spinning mill, now demolished.

The Trust formed to administrate the Marsden, Guisburn and Long Preston Turnpike consisted of over two hundred local gentlemen whose duties included the collection of tolls and the management of road repairs in the area. This house was built in 1805 and functioned until 1872 when the Trust was dissolved and the gates were removed. In 1841 and 1851 the census returns show that the toll collector was also the village postmaster and postman. In later years the position was held at one stage by a tailor, and at another by a shoemaker. As in other parts of the country the turnpike system was accused of not recognising the needs of local people who had to travel to and fro on a frequent basis, and this led to protests.

The toll house was built on Gisburn road adjacent to a bridge over Pendle Water, constructed to replace the packhorse bridge a little higher up the valley which had previously been the only means of crossing the Water. In 1982 the toll house was bought and refurbished by the Pendle Heritage Centre (now the Heritage Trust for the North West) and forms part of a group of heritage properties that includes the bridge and Park Hill, an old mansion house on the opposite bank of the river. The centre has exhibitions about the history of the area, including the story of the famous Pendle witches who were tried and executed in 1612. The toll house is leased out, and is not open to the public.

Steanor Bottom, Todmorden, Lancashire

1821 – GRADE II* LISTED
TOLL HOUSE NATIONAL ID YW.SBO

New spinning mills built astride fast flowing streams meant a rapid development of industry in previously completely rural areas. This house occupies a commanding position on the north-south road between Manchester, Burnley and Halifax, and is one of the few that retains the toll board that gave legal backing to the charges levied by its toll keeper.

The board gives a good idea of the forms of transport used in those days, including horse-drawn carriages, wagons of various types, and driven livestock. From a reading of the list of tolls set out it will be apparent that calculation and imposition of a toll would, in some cases, take a while to impose, and be subject to dispute.

Nearby is a canal, one of a network greatly used until the roads were improved.

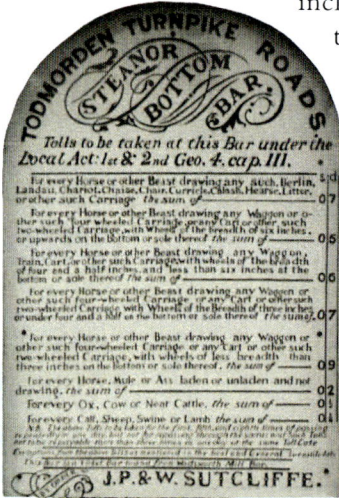

74

Spaniards Inn, Hampstead Heath, London

19TH CENTURY - GRADE II LISTED
TOLL HOUSE NATIONAL ID   LO.HAM

The small building on the right of the picture was used as a toll house, marking the entry to the estate of the Bishop of London. Although situated opposite a very famous public house, its position on a sharp bend of a very busy road makes it inconspicuous. It is incredible that it has survived at such a constricted point. In 1967 it was restored with funds raised by the Hampstead Heath Protection Society and was presented to the Greater London Council to hold in perpetuity.

Many famous people, including Charles Dickens, have been associated with the Inn and Hampstead.

Blackstone Edge, Littleborough, Manchester

19TH CENTURY - GRADE II LISTED
TOLL HOUSE NATIONAL ID   LA.LIT01

The first turnpike road in this bleak, moorland district was the Blackstone Edge Old Road, built in 1765, which is now little more than a track across the turf and a few hollows. The old coach road was superseded twenty years later by a faster, better graded one from Rochdale to Halifax and this cut across the Old Road. At the junction lies the Stormer Hill Bar Cottage, a former toll house, barely noticeable to the traffic that passes by at speed on the hill. This low, stone building was erected on the junction of the Old and New Blackstone roads to prevent the evasion of tolls by travellers over the moorland tracks.

At the top of the hill is an inn where additional horses were added to the teams hauling coaches up the steep gradients which Daniel Defoe described as 'very frightful, narrow and deep, with a hollow precipice on the right that made it very dangerous'.

The old packhorse route over Blackstone Edge was used by travellers over the Pennines for centuries, and nearby there is to be seen the remains of a paved roadway extending over the moors for about two miles which is thought may be attributed to the Romans. There is an interesting central trough along the centre of the paving which may have been for drainage or, if it was filled with turf, would have given a better foothold for the horses. It's also possible that this could have been part of a primitive winching system for hauling coaches up the steep incline.

Setchey, Norfolk

19TH CENTURY - NOT GRADED
TOLL HOUSE NATIONAL ID NO.NRU

Records indicate this toll house at Setchey, near Kings Lynn, was built at the height of the turnpike and coaching boom of the 1830s, but there are few others to be seen in the county.

The original cost of building this house, together with another at North Runcton, with their 'gates', was put at £700. The building is faced with carstone, known locally as 'gingerbread' stone on account of its extraordinary yellow-brown colour which is due to the presence of iron oxide. It can be carved into smooth-faced blocks, and was quarried in nearby Snettisham and Heacham. These two quarries supplied stone for stabilising the navigation channels around the Wash.

Daniel Defoe, on his travels, found nearby Kings Lynn a 'rich and populous, thriving port-town', dealing mainly in coal and wine.

Whitfield, Northumberland

19TH CENTURY - GRADE II LISTED
TOLL HOUSE NATIONAL ID   NB PLE

'Toll Cottage' is situated on a tight bend adjacent to a high river bridge on the road between Alston and Hexham in one of the most beautiful areas close to Hadrian's Wall and the historic village of Blanchland.

The high moorland surroundings were intensively mined for a variety of minerals but the workings have fallen into disuse in modern times, and it is now a mainly pastoral county.

Littleborough, Nottinghamshire

19TH CENTURY - GRADE II LISTED
TOLL HOUSE NATIONAL ID - NOT LISTED

In the midst of open farmland and dwarfed by huge chimneys and numerous pylons this toll house was built on a turnpike road which was extended from Retford by a circuitous route in 1825. The road terminates in a small cluster of houses with a Norman church on the bank of the river Trent. Here, during a severe drought in 1933, the remains of a Roman ford were exposed. The road is believed to have been in regular use up until recent times and was turnpiked in the 19th century.

John Loudon Mcadam was one of three outstanding men responsible for road-making during this historic period. His system of road surfacing was for broken stones to be laid to a depth of about ten inches, which would then be consolidated. The Trustees of the Sheffield-Glossop, Retford-Littleborough Ferry, Grantham-Nottingham and Leadenham Hill-Mansfield turnpikes consulted Mcadam with regard to his methods and these were put into operation to improve conditions in the area.

This lonely house now seems to epitomise the rise and decline of industry in some parts of the country. What would have been quite a busy road has become isolated and redundant, yet symbolises part of our history.

Botley, Oxfordshire

19TH CENTURY - NOT GRADED
TOLL HOUSE NATIONAL ID   OX.OXF03

No traveller in the 16th and 17th century going northwards along the Great North Road would leave London without first priming his pistols! Passengers boarding at Alconbury and journeying by mail coach or stage coach would hide their watches and jewellery between their skin and underclothes, for Alconbury Hill was notorious as a robbing place, almost as well known as Gads Hill near Rochester, Hounslow Heath and Finchley Common. Between the 64th and 65th milestones from London was a deep, solitary hollow at the foot of a northward slope, shut in by dense woods, named Stonegate Hole. When the road was lowered in later years many human bones were found there, supposedly the remains of unfortunate travellers who had been killed by thieves and highwaymen.

Outside the Old Gate House Inn (now the White House) at Botley used to hang a sign showing a masked 'dodger of tolls' and a furious gate keeper raising his fist in frustration outside his modest house. The main route out of Oxford to the West was through Botley and thence over a bridge at Eynsham where a toll is still collected.

The White House was closed for two years from 2007, but has now been renovated and reopened.

Dorchester, Oxfordshire

1815 - GRADE II LISTED
TOLL HOUSE NATIONAL ID OX.DOR

This is a delightful survivor standing in the lee of the Abbey church in an historic village. The building is a curious design, providing woefully inadequate accommodation by modern standards, yet at one time it housed a family with three children! Latterly it has been a shop and an office. It is thought to be contemporary with a 'new' bridge over the Thames erected in 1815 on this old established route between Oxford and Wallingford, happily now diverted. In addition to the ancient Abbey buildings behind it there remain a number of mediaeval timber houses and coaching inns in the main street.

Farming dominated the village and gave occupation to millers, corn dealers, butchers, wheelwrights and blacksmiths. In the 1840s two coaches, the Defiance and the Rival, left the White Hart for Oxford in one direction, and London in the other, twice a day.

Kidlington, Oxfordshire

19TH CENTURY - GRADE II LISTED
TOLL HOUSE NATIONAL ID   OX.OXF03

This was formerly known as the Old Man's Gate Toll House. Looked at in isolation this appears to be a fine house, with its stone 'eyebrows' and lintels, yet this double-fronted toll house is not only on a busy road but is now almost engulfed by the ever expanding city of Oxford.

Turnpikes in and around Oxford mushroomed, and it is said that following the Great Fire of London roads through the county were severely tested by the enormous loads of timber and stone required for the rebuilding.

Oxford was an important destination, or staging post, for coaches, and at the height of their era as many as a hundred would arrive every day. The organisation and business to support such movement can only be imagined, ranging from inns to grooms, horses and farriers. The toll keepers would have been extremely busy.

An Ordnance Survey map of 1878 shows a weighing engine on the opposite side of the road to the toll house.

Blists Hill, Telford, Shropshire

1829 (REBUILT 1972) - NOT GRADED
TOLL HOUSE NATIONAL ID SA.GOR03

Designed by the famous road engineer, Thomas Telford, the Shelton Toll House formerly stood on the London to Holyhead road a mile north of Shrewsbury but in 1972 was taken down and re-located in a simulated setting in this outdoor museum. It has been placed in a lonely lane with an iron 'sunray' gate barring the way through, reminiscent of conditions two hundred years ago. Inside, the house has been furnished in an appropriate style and staffed to portray life as it would have been experienced during the 18th and 19th centuries.

Blists Hill is part of the Ironbridge Gorge World Heritage Site; it is situated in a remarkable valley, arguably the birthplace of the Industrial Revolution. Nearby there are huge furnaces and kilns for the manufacture of iron and china, and the river is spanned by the impressive Iron Bridge, at the end of which is another toll house exhibiting its scale of charges outside.

Cockshutt, Shropshire

NOT GRADED
TOLL HOUSE NATIONAL ID - NOT LISTED

This tiny cottage sits at a minor road junction in a small village in rural Shropshire and was, no doubt, converted for use as a toll house from an existing house. Its name 'Catch-um-all Cottage' needs little explanation, and is a delightful reminder of previous use and probable annoyance for the local farming community.

Ludlow, Temeside, Shropshire

19TH CENTURY - GRADE II LISTED
TOLL HOUSE NATIONAL ID   SA.LUD07

In mediaeval times this delightful and much-visited border town was the capital of the Welsh Marches and is still dominated by the 11th-century castle which stands on a bluff above the river Teme. The town is full of handsome Tudor and Georgian buildings, the best known of which is probably the richly timbered Feathers Hotel, while the Old Angel was an important coaching inn.

The toll house pictured here built by the Second Ludlow Turnpike Trust retains a quite distinctive character, although its immediate surroundings do nothing to enhance its historical importance. At the time of photographing, the building appeared to be empty and semi-derelict but is now inhabited. The pointed arches are an interesting feature, while the recess for a toll board is clear.

Montford Bridge, Shropshire
19TH CENTURY - GRADE II LISTED
TOLL HOUSE NATIONAL ID   SA.MOF

One of the Telford-designed toll houses near Shrewsbury, this has the standard octagonal shape with conical roof and projecting porch, and it adjoins a crossing of the river Severn. Nowadays the London to Holyhead road, so triumphantly re-engineered by Thomas Telford in the early 19th century, bypasses this spot on a new bridge, leaving the toll house in a peaceful backwater just a few miles outside the town.

Shrewsbury has many old properties and much history. Centred on a castle site surrounded by a loop in the river, it was probably the ease of defence that brought the town into being, and many ancient buildings are testimony to its occupation over the years. Being situated on an important trading and passenger highway, on the route to Ireland, brought it into great prominence. The toll keeper at Montford Bridge would have been a very busy person!

Daniel Defoe said of Shrewsbury:

Here is a great market for Welch flannel which the factors buy up of the poor Welch people, who manufacture it, and thence it is sent to London; and it is a very considerable manufacture indeed thro' all this part of the country, by which the poor are very profitably employ'd.

Here I was showed a very visible and remarkable appearance of the great ancient road or way called Watling Street which comes from London to this town and goes on hence to the utmost coast of Wales; where it crossed the Severn there are remains of a stone bridge to be seen in the bottom of the river, when the water is low.

Ruyton XI Towns, Shropshire

19TH CENTURY - NOT GRADED
TOLL HOUSE NATIONAL ID SA.PLA

The little town of Ruyton XI Towns was formed in 1300 by uniting eleven townships, and Ruyton was important enough in the Middle Ages to have the dignity of being a borough. This borough status was rescinded in 1886 and although there is now still a thriving community here, Ruyton XI Towns is now classified as a village. This uniquely rounded toll house would have served the road crossing the river Perry (between Shrewsbury and Oswestry) and, like the old river bridge and many of the houses, the toll house is built of random red sandstone blocks. Listed in the National Toll House register as Platt Bridge.

Wrockwardine, Shropshire

1835 - GRADE II LISTED
TOLL HOUSE NATIONAL ID SA.WRO02

This house at Burcot near Wrockwardine has a most interesting feature - to the right of the usual projection on to the road is a very unusual halved door, with striking ornamental ironwork, shown above. A few years ago the then occupant spoke of a visit they'd had from a relative of the last toll keeper, and one is left to wonder what tales he could have divulged about the conditions of the roads in Shropshire in the 19th century. This building is an excellent example of a Telford design, on the old A5 between Telford and Shrewsbury.

The new town of Telford developed in the 1960s from an amalgamation of several places including Coalport and Coalbrookdale, Madeley and Ironbridge, to commemorate the talented man whose bridges, viaducts, canals and roads are still to be seen everywhere in this area. Hundreds of old mine shafts had to be sealed and much landscaping and removal of pit mounds took place to enable the transformation into a thriving community. The Ironbridge Gorge Museum has helped to preserve the history of the area.

Bath (Pulteney Bridge), Somerset

1773 (REBUILT CIRCA 1800) - GRADE I LISTED
TOLL HOUSE NATIONAL ID - NOT LISTED

Named after William Pulteney, 1st Earl of Bath, the bridge on which this building stands was designed by Robert Adam in 1770 and built by 1773. It was inspired by the Pontevecchio in Florence and is lined with shops on both sides. The toll house, with its cupola on the roof, is at the end of the bridge terrace. Clearly the turnpike route over Pulteney Bridge was an important one. Bath took its name and its fame from the therapeutic waters, the qualities of which were known to the Roman invaders who constructed elaborate baths and temples. These were rediscovered in excavations, together with a bronze head of Minerva, the Roman god of healing, and a revived interest in the spa led to Bath becoming a mecca for high society out of London, especially as it was also on the route to Bristol. This led to a spate of building, as seen in the elegant Nash residences erected in the 18th century in the city centre.

The Great Bath, when it was discovered, was found to be lined with lead which had been moulded by the Romans 2000 years ago, and it was fed by springs far below which produce 500,000 gallons of water at a constant temperature of 49 degrees. Sam Weller, one of Dickens' characters, described the water as 'tasting like warm flat-irons'.

Quarries two miles south, at Coombe Down, provided the stone for a city of classical beauty. Many houses bear plaques recording the names of famous residents of the past - John Wesley, Lord Nelson, Thomas Gainsborough and Emperor Napoleon of France. Despite royal patronage in the 17th century, Bath became notorious for pick-pockets, duellers, gamblers and quack doctors, until the arrival of 'Beau' Nash made it more respectable.

The photograph below is of an equally stylish booth on the nearby bridge, North Parade.

Bruton, Somerset

19TH CENTURY - GRADE II LISTED
TOLL HOUSE NATIONAL ID   SO.BRU01

There are two toll houses at opposite ends of this small town which is very ancient in origin. Celtic, Roman and Dark Age sites have been found on hills nearby. In past years the town had active wool and silk industries but no working mills remain today. Bruton is compact, and this applies also to this toll house which stands at a road junction on a hill out of the town leading to Frome. The decorative gable boards are an attractive feature. It would appear that the road level has been raised since it was built as the porch is now below the pavement.

This Deed, dated 1876, shows that the sale of this house into private hands, was for the sum of £40, in the reign of 'His Late Majesty, King William the Fourth'.

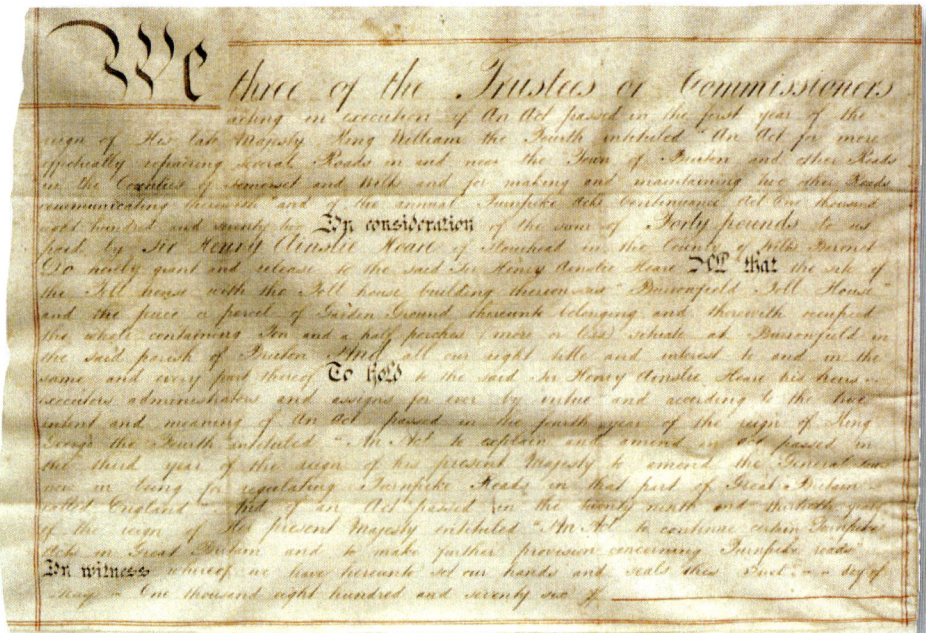

Chard, Somerset

19TH CENTURY - GRADE II LISTED
TOLL HOUSE NATIONAL ID SO.CHA01

With its studded door, gothic windows, thatched roof, knapped flints and timber poles, this very characterful old dwelling stands at a junction of two roads where a dog-leg road improvement with lesser incline was constructed. Originally built on the Yeovil to Honiton Turnpike the building has now been renovated for accommodation.

Several turnpike roads converged on Chard which was at the centre of an agricultural area. One of these roads is called 'Catch Gate Lane', possibly a reference to those trying to escape the Snowdon Hill Turnpike, but it could have related to any one of a number of toll houses then ringing the town.

Chard had a thriving wool industry for hundreds of years until in the 19th century local people began making the netting from which machine-made lace is produced. Benefiting from a raised location, 400 feet above sea level, Chard is an attractive town with a mile-long main street and many fine buildings.

Ilminster, Somerset

19TH CENTURY - GRADE II LISTED
TOLL HOUSE NATIONAL ID SO.ILM02

As in many of the buildings in the town and surrounding villages, this house is built of mellow Ham stone and has an overhanging gable which shows the iron fixings for the tollboard (long gone).

For centuries Ilminster was involved in the wool trade, but this has now been replaced by a variety of businesses including clothing and agricultural machinery. Fortunately for the town, the main London to Exeter road has been diverted from the high street, at the eastern end of which is another former toll house, of different design.

North Street (Ashton Gate), Bristol, Somerset

1820 - GRADE II LISTED
TOLL HOUSE NATIONAL ID   BRI01

This stylish Georgian toll house at the junction of Coronation Road and North Street is close to the centre of Bristol, formerly Britain's third-ranking seaport, renowned for its monopoly of the West Indies trade in slaves, its exports of wool and imports of wines from Spain, Portugal and France. The city grew up around its port on the river Avon, and ships sailed to America with emigrants and for trade from the 15th century. Bristol became a thriving centre with a web of good highways radiating to all parts of the kingdom. Isambard Kingdom Brunel's steamships *Great Western* (1837) and *Great Britain* (1843) were launched from Bristol but were later forced to ply from Liverpool because of high charges imposed by the Docks Committee. Brunel redesigned the docks in 1830 and was commissioned to build the suspension bridge to span the Avon Gorge at Clifton.

The expression 'paying on the nail' is believed to be related to the four bronze pillars ('nails') outside the old Bristol Exchange building, on which merchants concluded their money transactions.

South Cheriton, Somerset

1824 - GRADE II LISTED
TOLL HOUSE NATIONAL ID SO.HOR

Dating from 1824 this is one of the few remaining examples of a toll house that still exhibits its original tariff board. The porch projects on to the road and the side windows give a good view in each direction for the keeper to watch out for approaching vehicles or people.

Yeovil, a short distance away, was the centre of the glove and leather industry from the 14th century, and this toll house is in a pretty conservation village on the road from Wincanton to Blandford Forum and Poole.

Stanton Drew, Bristol, Somerset

19TH CENTURY - GRADE II LISTED
TOLL HOUSE NATIONAL ID SO.STA

This quaint, almost fairytale toll house, has been beautifully maintained but is situated on a very busy road south of Bristol, in an area where there were many toll gates 150 years ago. Several toll houses remain but none of them compare to this example. It has a domed, thatched roof and gothic-style windows and the bracket for the tollboard can be seen, together with a letter collection box in the wall. It was strategically placed to guard each direction against toll evasion, but now it is perched precariously on a very small road island.

Nearby, in the village of Chew Magna, there are ancient remains of a triple circle of massive stones, while to the north is a view of Wansdyke, a massive earth bank of pre-Roman origins, stretching to Salisbury Plain.

Yeovil, Somerset

1854 - GRADE II LISTED
TOLL HOUSE NATIONAL ID   DO.BRA

This toll house is dwarfed by a large traffic island and an industrial estate on the A30 on the outskirts of Yeovil. The original function of this 'baronial-style' house might not be obvious to travellers today, yet it displays traditional features with its two-storey projection to give good views of approaching traffic. It has attractive tiling to the roof and unusual windows, and is built of stone similar to that of the adjacent bridge over the river Yeo.

Sicklesmere, Suffolk

19TH CENTURY - GRADE II LISTED
TOLL HOUSE NATIONAL ID SU.LIT

On the roadside between Sudbury and Bury St Edmunds, with a distinctive octagonal shape and a central chimney stack, this is a fine brick-built former toll house clearly showing the space for a list of charges for passing along the road and a neat shelter over what would have been the main door.

Although most of the wool industry collapsed in the 17th century in Suffolk, many of its skills were retained in the silk weaving industry in Sudbury and Braintree (in Essex).

Another industry which made this area famous was the raising of turkeys for London and surrounding counties. The birds were driven in huge droves on foot, sometimes numbering between three hundred and a thousand animals. The drive would begin in August when the harvest was almost complete so that they could feed on the stubble as they walked. The trade had to cease by the end of October when the roads became too muddy and churned for the birds' feet and legs to cope. Later a form of stacked cart was made to convey the live birds to London markets.

Chiddingfold, Surrey

19TH CENTURY - NOT GRADED
TOLL HOUSE NATIONAL ID SYCHI

In early days journeys through Surrey were notoriously difficult, if not dangerous, due to heavily wooded and wet soils, and attacks by highwaymen. Improvements brought about under turnpike legislation eased travelling considerably between London and ports in the south; eminent sailors including Drake and Nelson used these routes and the coaching inns. In considering the turnpiking of the Godalming to Duncton route Parliament heard of the difficulties and expense of improving existing holloways and chose an alternative route via Milford. Often the gentry influenced decisions because of the impact on their estates and their personal convenience. Existing driftways and holloways were widened into cartways, and those routes serving a market town had to be at least eight feet wide.

The Round House at Chiddingfold, formerly called the Winterton Toll House, is now situated snugly below the level of the road and it is not easy to see all its features. The brick construction is somewhat unusual, especially the decorative studded mortar used in the walling, called 'garretting' and the contrasting brickwork over the door and lower windows. It is not clear when the house was built but as the toll board (preserved in the Haslemere Museum) refers to steam power, it may date from the mid-19th century. A previous owner believed the garden had been divided into quarters with hedging for use as a cattle pound for those travellers who were unable to pay their toll fines.

In nearby Chiddingfold village the Crown Inn dates from the 13th century when it was used as a place to stay for pilgrims and monks. It claims to have the oldest licence in Surrey and one of the oldest in the country, and is regarded as a particularly fine example of a mediaeval timber-framed building.

Clapham, Sussex

1820 - GRADE II LISTED
TOLL HOUSE NATIONAL ID SXW.CLA

A carefully graded road sweeps down the chalk hills of the South Downs behind Worthing, and modern travellers might not notice this unusual building as they pass by on the busy road. The Long Furlong Toll House was built in gothic style, possibly dictated by a local landowner in the early 19th century. It lies on the road from London to the south coast near Cissbury Ring. This curious, castellated house formerly had one room downstairs with another above, probably reached by a ladder in one of the turrets. Above the central window there is an arched opening where the tollboard would have displayed the charges for passing through the gate.

Lindfield, Sussex

17TH CENTURY - GRADE II LISTED
TOLL HOUSE NATIONAL ID SXW.LIN01

Lindfield's main street is lined with characterful houses, and at one end is a village pond and pleasant open green. No. 56, now a shop, is a 17th-century building on a timber frame which, in turnpike days apparently functioned as a toll house until the day came when the gate was removed in 1884. A modern commemorative plaque marks the spot where the gate was removed, and below that in the stonework can be seen the older stone inscribed with the date.

Shoreham, Sussex

1833 - GRADE II LISTED
TOLL HOUSE NATIONAL ID   SXW.SHO

In the 17th century Sussex roads were renowned as some of the worst and most difficult for journeying, and coaches had to be abandoned in deep and muddy ruts. The coastal road linking Brighton to Chichester came comparatively late in relation to routes inland as these and other towns developed only when communications improved with London.

When Daniel Defoe visited Shoreham he described it as 'A seafaring town and chiefly inhabited by ship carpenters and chandlers and all the several trades depending on the building and fitting up of ships which is their chief business'. He commented that the river on which the town stood was navigable by boats big enough to convey the large timbers needed from the wooded country inland, but shingle accumulated and cramped the harbour entrance. The river Adur was a main artery into the Weald from the coast. Many buildings in this area of Sussex are of weather-boarding, probably using continental softwood imported through Shoreham harbour.

A very different architectural style is displayed in this toll house, with its attractive dentil ribbing and roof with parapets. It is at the eastern end of the Norfolk Bridge over the estuary of the river Adur, and was built in 1833 to complement the design of an earlier bridge, built at that time - the Norfolk Suspension Bridge. The 1833 bridge superseded the timber toll road built in 1781 and reconstructed in 1916. This bridge, shown below was used for cars until 1970 but has now been renovated for use as a pedestrian walkway. It is overlooked by the fine Lancing College Chapel, and also by Shoreham Airport. Yet another modern bridge, the Adur Flyover, now carries through-traffic high over the river.

The original Shoreham toll bridge, further upstream than the Norfolk bridge, was built in 1781. This was replaced by this bridge of the same design in 1916.

The toll house (above) and the Norfolk suspension bridge, were built in 1833. The bridge was replaced by a string girder bridge in 1922 (in turn replaced by a new concrete box girder bridge in 1987).

St Leonards, Sussex

1830 - NOT GRADED
TOLL HOUSE NATIONAL ID SXE.STL

On the Maze Hill Road approach to the town, towers a unique arched gateway, built about 1830, over a former turnpike road on a route that was superseded after only a few years. The right-hand side of the structure is still known as 'The Toll House', and under the arch there are indications of a former doorway which may have been used by a gate keeper. North Lodge, on the other side, bears a plaque commemorating it as a former residence of Sir Henry Rider Haggard, author.

Ticehurst, Sussex

1762 - GRADE II LISTED
TOLL HOUSE NATIONAL ID SXE.TIC01

Heavy soil and thickly wooded areas made communication extremely difficult in parts of the south, but in the late 18th century there were a number of toll houses established on turnpike roads within a ten-mile radius of Ticehurst.

This pretty weather-boarded cottage is sited at the junction of the High Street (the B2099) and Three Leg Cross Road in this Wealden village. Another toll house in the village was built for the same Trust but is of different design.

Arrow, Warwickshire

CIRCA 1810 - GRADE II LISTED
TOLL HOUSE NATIONAL ID WA.ARR

Prominently located at the junction of two roads and close to the ancient town of Alcester, this toll house shows a twin aspect with space over the door-ways (one of which has been removed) for the board of charges. It was built around 1760 and would have been in an important position for exacting dues because of its proximity to the growing industry in the country south of Birmingham. It was stylishly built, with double windows and 'eyebrows' to decorate windows, doors and tollboards, but now seems dwarfed by surrounding buildings.

Alcester has strong Roman connections as it lies off Ryknild (or Icknield) Street - the road that runs from Bourton-on-the-Water northwards to Birmingham and Derby, and eastwards to Stratford-on-Avon.

Stratford-Upon-Avon, Warwickshire

1814 - GRADE I LISTED
TOLL HOUSE NATIONAL ID WA.STR

Dating from the 19th century and situated at one of the most important and spectacular entrances to the town on one of the multiple arches of the bridge, this squat polygon held a dramatic position in former days on the Clopton Bridge across the river Avon. The Clopton family lived at Clopton House near Stratford from the 1220s, and Hugh Clopton became Lord Mayor of London and gave the town its stone bridge and also the nave of the Guild Chapel.

Aldbourne, Wiltshire

1814 – GRADE II LISTED
TOLL HOUSE NATIONAL ID WI.ALD01

This very attractive, thatched toll cottage has been in private ownership for many years. It is on the Swindon to Hungerford road which passes through rolling downland and a pretty valley. The low-arched doorway, with windows on each side, is almost hidden beneath the overhanging thatch.

The nearby village of Aldbourne was famous for its bell foundry and for its willow- and straw-plaiting industry.

Box, Wiltshire

19TH CENTURY - GRADE II LISTED
TOLL HOUSE NATIONAL ID WI.BOX02

This attractive, stone-faced house - the Kingsdown Toll House - lies on a quiet lane now, yet it used to see busier times when it was facing the old coach road from London to Bath, notorious for highwaymen and footpads. On a dark night it is easy to imagine such dangers still exist beneath the trees in quiet, country areas such as this. The old doorway has been replaced with a window and what is now a blank alcove above would have displayed the charges for use of the road.

Evidence of the Industrial Revolution can be seen nearby where the huge tunnel portal, built by Brunel, used Bath stone for monumental masonry.

Devizes, Wiltshire

CIRCA 1840 – GRADE II LISTED
TOLL HOUSE NATIONAL ID WI.DEV01

This fine building, with battlements, is triple-fronted and lies on a very restricted site at the junction of two very busy roads. It was built c.1840 and bears the name 'Shanes Castle'.

The name 'Devizes' is said to be a corruption of 'Division' where, on the London to Bath road the Roman and Celtic districts met. Nearby is the Kennet and Avon Canal which would have been used to transport goods from the silk factories, and its twenty-nine locks between the town of Devizes and Calne have been restored for public use in recent years.

The following report from the *Illustrated London News* of 1868 gives an interesting insight into the reaction of locals to the abolition of toll gates:

A grand popular Festival took place at Devizes last week to celebrate the abolition of Toll Gates in that neighbourhood. On the evening of Saturday 31st the last day of the Tolls, just before midnight, a band of music went round to all the gates, playing various airs at each and concluding with the National Anthem . . . the Gates purchased at the sale of the Turnpike Trust property . . . Were immolated on a bonfire built of an immense pile of faggots . . . A great crowd of people . . . Blaze visible for many miles around.

Broadway, Worcestershire

19TH CENTURY - GRADE II LISTED
TOLL HOUSE NATIONAL ID WO.BRW

Villages and towns of the Cotswolds have an architectural uniformity of which inhabitants and visitors never tire. The colour of the mellow limestone used to build houses, and the simple styles, has attracted tourists for a long time. Roofs are tiled with graded slates which weather to a soft grey when covered with moss and lichens.

Broadway's main street has now been bypassed to accommodate the heavy traffic of the tourist season, but one historical building at the foot of the hill is a reminder of days when coaches of another kind clogged the thorough-fare and cottagers would have been accustomed to the sounds of cattle herds passing through.

The design of this house is not unusual except for the projecting bay window beside the entrance door from which a toll keeper could espy the approaching wagons and stage coaches which would be preparing for, or recovering from, the rigours of the very steep hill above Broadway.

Droitwich, Worcestershire

19TH CENTURY - GRADE II LISTED
TOLL HOUSE NATIONAL ID WO.DRO

The first Turnpike Act between Droitwich and Worcester was passed in 1713 following complaints that the road was impractical for carrying salt for nine months in the year. For many hundreds of years salt was one of the most essential commodities to be transported all over the country for use as a preservative - the mediaeval equivalent of the refrigerator. Springs beneath the ancient town of Droitwich were said to be ten times saltier than ordinary sea water, and the Romans called the town 'Salinae'. Main supplies of salt came from Cheshire (as mentioned in the *Domesday Book*), but it is believed salt in this area came from an extension of the main field deposited during the Triassic period when it was covered by a shallow sea. In very early days salt was used as a currency or as an exchange standard, as it contained very few impurities.

Droitwich was the focus of a number of routes as it was accessible from the river Severn, and many of them were turnpiked, including the saltway leading east to Stratford on Avon.

This house is unique in its elevational treatment with its recessed, full-height arches and contrasting painted panels. It flanks a road named 'Holloway', a description often given to an old route used by travellers and wagons when, because years of use by horses and wheeled vehicles wore down the soil to rock bottom, the way became several feet below the general level of the land. William Cobbett and Gilbert White both wrote about 'holloways' they had seen on their travels.

Droitwich developed into a spa in the early 19th century when 'taking the waters' became fashionable, with its brine baths and hotels.

118

Pershore, Worcestershire

19TH CENTURY - GRADE II LISTED
TOLL HOUSE NATIONAL ID WO.PER01

The river Avon flows by this prosperous Georgian town in the famous fruit-growing area, the Vale of Evesham. From the modern bridge can be seen an ancient, six-arched mediaeval bridge and, situated close by is this brick toll house. The original board with its tariffs has been replaced by a modern version that makes interesting reading.

The cathedral city of Worcester is a few miles away and is a great tourist attraction, especially for the Royal Worcester Porcelain Works started by Dr Wall, a citizen anxious to restore the prosperity of the city following the decline of the cloth trade.

Ingleton, Yorkshire

CIRCA 1840 - GRADE II LISTED
TOLL HOUSE NATIONAL ID YN.ING

This small house, set at an angle to the road, afforded a view in both direc-
tions for the toll keeper and was erected in the early 19th century, together
with an inn opposite, when a new bridge over the river Greta was constructed
for the diverted turnpike. The original route had been along the narrow streets
of the village. The house is typical of the simple design used for several toll
houses on the Skipton to Kendal route.

Ingleton has been a popular venue for tourists and walkers, partly for its
quaintness but also because of the limestone caves and the waterfalls in the
Pennine hills to the north.

Middleham, Yorkshire

1830 – GRADE II LISTED
TOLL HOUSE NATIONAL ID YN.MID

The village of Middleham, formerly capital of Wensleydale and famous for its horse-breeding and racing establishments, is dominated by a Norman castle built circa 1170, which was formerly home to Richard, Duke of Gloucester, who later became Richard III. The castle has one of the largest keeps in England, and the town (mostly Georgian) has been made a Conservation Area.

In former days the river crossing, where the Ripon road is taken across the river Ure, was a very difficult one, so a simple suspension bridge was erected between pairs of castellated towers, with a simple cottage on the south side where tolls were collected. A year or so later this bridge collapsed under the weight of a herd of bullocks and had to be replaced. Tolls were charged to help with the upkeep of the repaired bridge, and it was later replaced by an iron girder one, retaining the original impressive towers which have become a feature in the beautiful moorland landscape.

In the photograph, the toll house is to the right of the bridge.

121

Ringinglow, Sheffield, Yorkshire

CIRCA 1778 - GRADE II LISTED
TOLL HOUSE NATIONAL ID YS.SHE02

This somewhat extraordinary structure stands at the junction of two roads leading to the moors high above Sheffield and was erected at the end of the 18th century when trustees were given powers to enclose land out of waste and draw stone from common quarries to construct a toll house near the Barberfields Cupola. This was a lead-smelting cupola where the lead was brought from Derbyshire and local coal was used for fuel. Later it was converted into a 'copperas' works, using this by-product of the local coal used in tanning.

The Barberfields Cupola Bar had a comparatively short life as a toll house and later became known as the Round House and was at one time owned by brewers from the Norfolk Arms opposite. The original door was at the junction of the two roads, allowing the keeper to attend to two separate gates. Many hexagonal structures built as toll houses were single story, which makes this one exceptional. The top floor was not habitable as it never had windows, nor a floor until more recently.

Sheffield was the centre of many packhorse routes, in particular from the saltfields of Cheshire. Then in the 1740s two nearly simultaneous inventions led to its development as a major industrial town; firstly, the crucible method of steel production using coke, and secondly the use of water power. It became renowned for the manufacture of cutlery from imported fine ores brought from Sweden via Hull, the Trent and Bawtry, then overland by packhorses. Steel was made from hard, refined iron with all its impurities removed. It is probable the local ore deposits were not of sufficient quality.

TOLL HOUSES
IN WALES

Llangollen, Clwyd

19TH CENTURY
TOLL HOUSE NATIONAL ID   NOT LISTED

Fronting the A5 road west of Llangollen and high above the river Dee valley is a Telford-style toll house at Ty Isaf, with a contemporary weigh house opposite (one of very few surviving examples).

One of the wonders of Wales, the elegant Pontcysyllte Aqueduct, is nearby and exemplifies the skill and ingenuity of the engineer, Thomas Telford. In 1793 the Ellesmere Canal Company wanted to build a canal to link the rivers Mersey, Dee and Severn but faced the major obstacles of various mine workings, hilly land and insufficient water. Telford's solution to the water issue was to construct the Horseshoe Falls on the river Dee at Llantysilio from where the build-up of water was guided into the canal which ran to Pontcysyllte. To ensure a regular supply, Lake Bala, from which the Dee flowed, was kept at a certain level from the end of the winter by a regulating weir. But how would he overcome the problem of carrying the canal over the wide Dee valley? It seemed an insurmountable problem, but not for Telford; he constructed a raised aqueduct 127 feet above the river, to be carried on eighteen piers of stone, the water to be carried in a cast-iron trough. It was an astonishing achievement and is still operational to this day.

The town of Llangollen is a short distance from Ty Isaf, and continues to host the International Eisteddfod annually.

Pumpsaint, Carmarthen, Dyfed

19TH CENTURY
TOLL HOUSE NATIONAL ID   NOT LISTED

A neat little structure with 'eyebrow' features, on the road between Lampeter and Llandovery, this small toll house lies on an old drove route through the Welsh mountains. 'Pumpsaint' is Welsh for 'Five Saints', a name derived from a nearby standing stone which has five sides.

Close by are Roman gold mines which were worked until 1939 and now are a tourist attraction under the auspices of the National Trust. The gold bullion produced is believed to have been transported to London by the drovers, and cattle were shod here for their long journey over the mountains to avoid payment of tolls on the roads.

Drovers are said to have initiated the first banks in which to hold their takings. The Bank of the Black Ox which was founded in 1799 in Llandovery gave rise eventually to Lloyds plc.

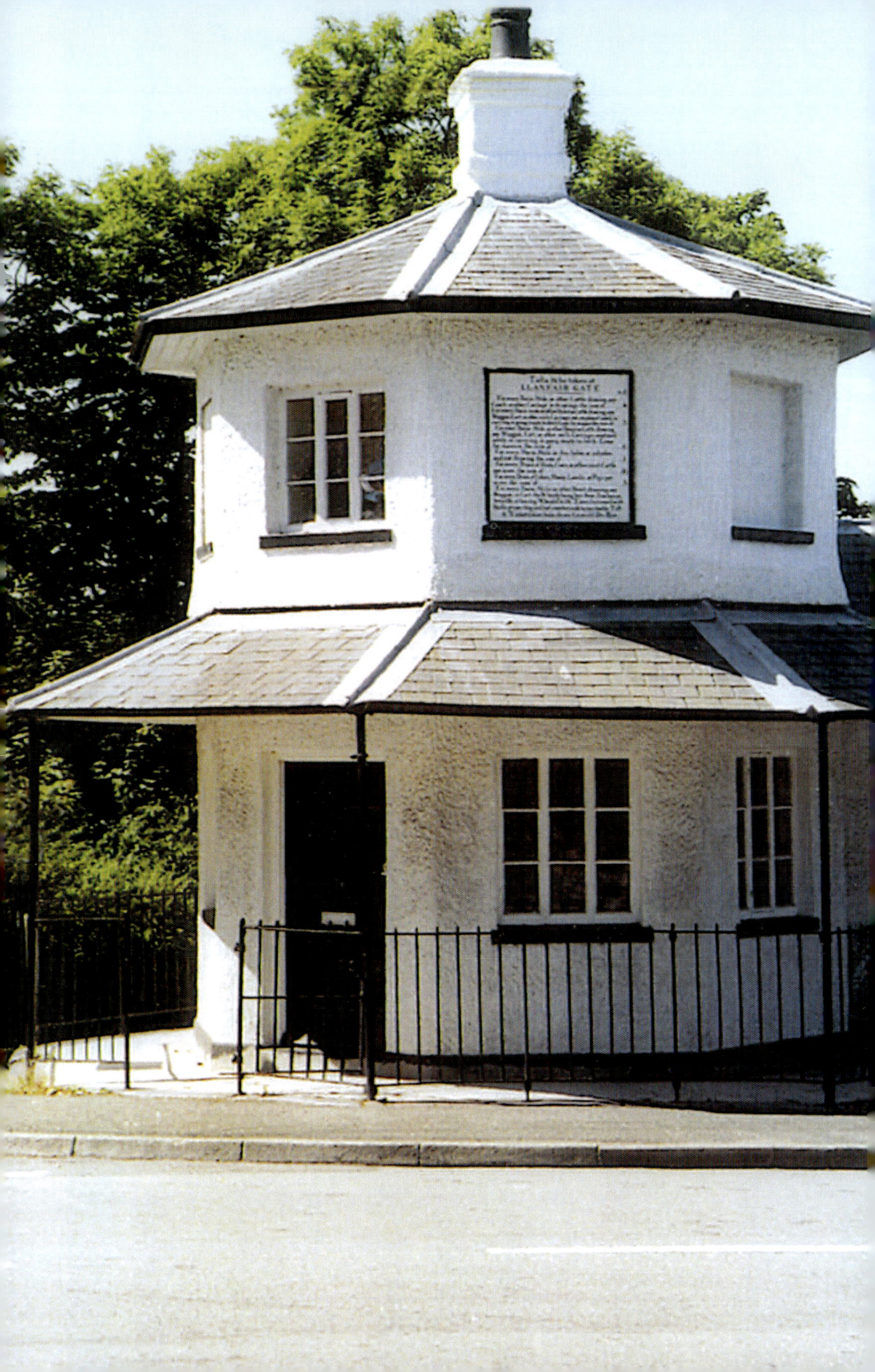
LLANFAIR GATE

Llanfair PG, Anglesey, Gwynedd

19TH CENTURY
TOLL HOUSE NATIONAL ID   NOT LISTED

The town where this building stands guard has grown up around this toll house and is known far and wide for its full Welsh name – the longest place name in Europe: Llanfairpwllgwyngyllgogerychwyrndrobwllllantysiliogogogoch.

Thomas Telford designed and supervised the building of the Menai Suspension Bridge, and the road from Holyhead on Anglesey to London. The bridge took him six years to build, from 1818 to 1826. To recover some of the vast amount spent on the bridge there were five toll gates, each with a toll house, that were erected at approximately five mile intervals between the Menai Suspension Bridge and Holyhead.

The first toll point was of course at the bridge itself, which is no longer in evidence. Toll houses still remain today at Llanfair Pwllgwyngyll (shown here), Gwalchmai, Caergeiliog (now a private dwelling), and at Penrhos, Holyhead (overleaf).

The Llanfair toll house was the first after the crossing of the Bridge on Telford's new Holyhead road. It stands at a junction with the road southwards to Plas Newydd. The design is similar to that of the other houses further along the route, with two storeys and has a galleried surround with a tollboard on both faces. It is a fine example still.

Tolls to be taken at
LLANFAIR GATE

Penrhos, Holyhead, Anglesey, Gwynedd

19TH CENTURY
TOLL HOUSE NATIONAL ID   NOT LISTED

This is a another example of a Telford–designed toll house. It has seen many different usages and when visited for the research for this book was a tea room The design is the same as the one at Llanfairpwllgwyngyll on the previous page. This toll house was taken down brick by brick and rebuilt just a few yards further back from its original position next to the road.

Porthmadog, Gwynedd (The 'Rebecca Toll Gate')

19TH CENTURY
TOLL HOUSE NATIONAL ID   NOT LISTED

This somewhat insignificant, small house is at the end of a long causeway carrying the busy A487 across the Afon Glaslyn estuary and marshes, saving a long detour around the estuary. The 'Cob' was built by William Maddocks between 1808 and 1811 and tolls were taken for almost two hundred years. In 2003, the Cob and toll house was bought by the Welsh Assembly and the final five pence toll was removed. This picture was taken when the tolls were still being taken. The old board in local slate is shown on the wall of the house, although the name of the gate is understood to be associated with a famous local sailing boat (pictured on the toll ticket) and not with the 19th century toll gate riots.

The causeway is crossed by the famous narrow gauge Ffestiniog Railway which was installed in 1836 to transport slate quarried in the hills at Blaenau down to the boats at Porthmadog. Now a tourist attraction, the little railway takes passengers through magnificent mountain scenery, and nearby is Portmeirion Village, creation of Clough Williams Ellis who was inspired to build a fantasy village in Italianate style and this has lent its name to a well-known range of china.

Mitchell Troy, Monmouthshire

19TH CENTURY
TOLL HOUSE NATIONAL ID   NOT LISTED

On a hilly road out of Monmouth this enlarged and modernised former toll house faces two roads and once had two doorways, each with side windows. It is probable there was considerable traffic passing by with coal from the mines in the Forest of Dean – a royal hunting preserve since Canute's day, and the first Forest Park in England.

Daniel Defoe wrote 'Near Monmouth the Duke of Beaufort has a fine seat called Troy . . . a most charming situation, seems to be much neglected'. The house is in a quiet area now, above the busy A40 trunk road.

Glasbury, Powys

19TH CENTURY
TOLL HOUSE NATIONAL ID   NOT LISTED

The old road now lies inside the fence fronting this cottage which is on the Brecon to Hereford route. Close to the lovely river Wye and to the English border, this is the area made famous by Reverend Kilvert in his *Diary*. He was for some years in the 19th century a curate in a nearby parish.

This building is built in a traditional style with its slate roof and projecting gable giving good vision of approaching traffic.

Hay on Wye nearby is well known these days as 'the largest second-hand bookshop in the world', with many of its shops involved in the trade.

Rhayader, Powys
19TH CENTURY
TOLL HOUSE NATIONAL ID NOT LISTED

Central Wales was much involved in riots against truly oppressive tolls in the mid-19th century because the people were very poor and felt it was unjust. Many of them rose up at night in order to destroy toll houses and toll gates in defiance of the authorities. It is suggested that this humble cottage survived because the toll keeper showed sympathy with the rioters. It lies on the south side of Rhayader.

Other historical features in the town have been demolished, such as the old market hall which had stood in the centre of the town since 1762 and has been replaced by a town clock and a war memorial.

Bibliography

Short History of Todmorden by J. Holden, Manchester University Press, 1912

The Norwich Road by Charles Harper, Chapman & Hall, 1901

The Drovers Roads of Wales by Shirley Toulson & Caroline Forbes, Wildwood House, 1977

Pembrokeshire Past & Present by Brian John, Greencroft Books, 1995

An Illustrated History of Coaches & Coaching by Ivan Sparkes, Spurbooks, 1975

Turnpikes & Toll-Bars - compiled by Mark Searle, Hutchinson, London, 1930

The Turnpike Road System in England 1663 - 1840 by W. Albert, Cambridge University Press, 1972

The Story of the Kings Highway by S. Webb, Longmans Green, 1913

The Turnpike Roads of Eighteenth Century Britain by E. Pawson, Academic Press, 1977

An Essex Turnpike Gate by John Copeland, Journal of Transport History, 1963

Bell's Life magazine

Patersons Roads by Daniel Paterson and Edward Mogg, Longman, 1826

Toone's Chronology, 1825

Gentleman's Magazine, 1749

Batsford Guide to Industrial Architecture of E. Anglia, 1980

Batsford Guide to Industrial Architecture of S.E. England, 1978

Batsford Guide to Industrial Architecture of West Midlands

Guide to England's Industrial Heritage by Keith Falconer, Batsford, 1980

Industrial Architecture of N.E. England by F. Atkinson

Wild Wales by George Borrow, John Murray, 1862

Roman Roads in Britain by Codrington, SPCK, 1903

Road Transport in Cumbria in 19th Century by L.A. Williams

The Peak District by K.C. Edwards, William Collins, 1962

Roads & Trackways of The Yorkshire Dales by Geoffrey Wright, Moorland Publishing, 1985

The Common Lands of England & Wales by W.G. Hoskins and L. Dudley Stamp, New Naturalist, 1963

William Cobbett's Rural Rides Revisited by Laurence Vulliamy, Pierrot Publishing, 1977

The Uncommercial Traveller by Charles Dickens, Chapman & Hall, 1861

Lost Trade Routes by Shirley Toulson, Shire, 1983

English Society in 18th Century by Roy Porter, Penguin Books, 1982